WEALTHIER TOGETHER

WEALTHIER TOGETHER

From Maximizing Short-Term Shareholder Value to Coevolution

HEINRICH ANKER

OPEN BOOK EDITIONS
A Berrett-Koehler Partner

iUniverse®

WEALTHIER TOGETHER
FROM MAXIMIZING SHORT-TERM SHAREHOLDER VALUE TO COEVOLUTION

iUniverse books may be ordered through booksellers or by contacting:

iUniverse
1663 Liberty Drive
Bloomington, IN 47403
www.iuniverse.com
1-800-Authors (1-800-288-4677)

ISBN: 978-1-4917-5659-1 (sc)
ISBN: 978-1-4917-5661-4 (hc)
ISBN: 978-1-4917-5660-7 (e)

Library of Congress Control Number: 2015902419

Translation of the German edition, titled
Ko-Evolution versus Eigennützigkeit. Creating Shared Value mit der Balanced Valuecard, Erich Schmidt Publishers, Berlin, June 2012
ISBN: 978-3-503-13886-9 (sc)
ISBN: 978-3-503-13887-6 (e)

Print information available on the last page.

iUniverse rev. date: 4/28/2015

For my wife, Verena, and
my daughter, Bettina

Contents

Preface

The paradigm of maximizing short-term gain has been around for several decades, and while it may have rationalized and systematized the economy for a certain time and been conducive to the welfare of businesses, today it represents a source of permanent crises and social, ecological, and economic threats to the economy and society, to people, and to the environment. The dogma according to which the pursuit of our own maximum benefit is supposed to contribute automatically to the greatest benefit of the greatest number, to the common good, is no longer scientifically tenable; it is merely another ideology.

> There is an alternative, a way out of the crisis, toward a better future for the economy and for society, and this is the way of coevolution. This book offers a pathway to this objective: the Value Balance in Business and creating shared value. The idea of creating shared value shows how companies can implement coevolution in their day-to-day business—a concept that demonstrates how service to society combines synergistically with the economic aspirations of the business and even gives the company a competitive edge.

However, a company can only develop the forward-looking potential of this concept if it is firmly established at all levels in its philosophy and culture of the company (i.e., on the level of consciousness, values, and attitudes and the associated motivation of the employees). The Value Balance in Business shows us the way through the concept of a pragmatic meaning- and performance-centered corporate philosophy and culture and its systematic development and maintenance, which forms the core of this book.

Creating shared value and the Value Balance in Business open a door to successful entrepreneurship in a new era of economic thinking and acting. Leading pioneer companies on all continents and of all sizes and ownership structures have been practicing this philosophy for many years with proven success that far exceeds the average. They acted and act beyond textbook economics and therefore have for a long time remained in the shadows. Now their time has come, and their genes will prevail. This book shows why this is so, and it aims to encourage as many businesses as possible to embark on the road to coevolution and lasting prosperity in the interests of customers, employees, society, the environment, and shareholders.

I am deeply grateful to Erich Schmidt Publishers, Berlin, for generously granting me the publication rights in English as well as to the many representatives from business and academia whose critical inputs have—knowingly or not—made it possible to develop the concept of a meaning- and performance-centered corporate philosophy and culture.

Heinrich Anker, November 2014
anker[at]pop.agri.ch

1. Introduction

If your actions inspire others to dream
more, learn more, do more and
become more, you are a leader.
                    —John Quincy Adams, the sixth
                        president of the United States

Traditional Utilitarian Economic Philosophy and Practice Has Had Its Day

Over the past thirty years, we have been witness to a string of economic crises occurring at ever-shorter intervals. Violent global shocks coursing through the economy are increasingly also shaking the foundations of the civil societies affected by the process, creating a growing divide between business and society. The continuously widening income and wealth inequality that we see in so many national economies is making this divide even larger.

At the same time, the number of employees who feel less and less connected with their work and their employers is steadily increasing— the gulf between companies and their employees is widening, and rigorous cost savings and the associated reduction of benefits are likewise opening a chasm between businesses and their customers.

The emergence of these crises and distortions is not primarily the result of inopportune economic constellations; the causes lie deeper, in traditional economic thinking and acting itself: the dogma of the standard and mainstream theory of economics, that maximizing one's own (short-term) benefit or profit leads to the greatest common good. This theory has proved to be untenable. To put it in its own terminology, it is inefficient.

Heinrich Anker

Outlines of a New Enterprise Philosophy and Culture

This book does not merely criticize these issues but attempts to open the door to a new approach to economic thinking and acting on a theoretical and practical level. The central points of departure are corporate philosophy and culture: they constitute the link between employees and companies on the one hand and between companies, customers, and both society and the natural environment on the other.

As empirical research demonstrates ever more clearly, corporate culture is a highly relevant independent factor in the performance and robustness of a company, yet many education curricula still do not afford it nearly its rightful role. This is because there is a myriad of methods to identify corporate culture and correlate it directly with a company's success. However, many of these approaches are merely descriptive and are not very helpful. Statistical correlations between certain types of corporate cultures and the company's success do not say anything specific about the real reasons for this connection, and it is therefore difficult to develop and sustain a high-performance corporate culture based on these approaches. Best practice comparisons and external benchmarking in the field of corporate culture are of no real help, either.

Back to Fundamentals—Looking for a New Motivation Theory

That is why this book starts with the most fundamental approach: it establishes and develops the concept of a meaning- and performance-centered philosophy and culture, firstly out of the company's purpose to provide services and secondly out of humanity's basic needs—in other words, our existential needs. These will be examined in the context of philosophical anthropology, meaning-oriented psychology, and neuro- and evolutionary biology. The first existential need that we will consider is man's desire for meaning—that fundamental desire that we humans have for insight into the meaning of our actions and our functions. The second is our need for recognition as human beings; this is the source of our individual identity and the sense that we have a place in life, that our existence has meaning—meaning as opposed to futility.

2

These needs are this fundamental because they are the basic attributes that raise humans to the status of human beings—they constitute our humanity. Our will and our power to mobilize our resources are strongest when these needs are fed. If you require people to perform, you have to offer them opportunities to experience meaning and recognition in return.

From Motivation Theory to Enterprise Philosophy and Culture

The next question that needs to be answered is, how should a corporate philosophy and culture be designed in order to fulfill these existential needs, thus in turn providing the company with a strong potential for performance? The core idea is this: research shows that, according to key indicators, companies that consistently serve their clients and society above all else are, in the long run, six to nine times more profitable than companies that subordinate everything else to short-term self-interest or profit maximization. This has nothing to do with romantic notions of business—there are good reasons why this is so.

From Philosophy and Culture to High-Enterprise Performance and Lasting Success

The first and most important reason is that companies that primarily focus on serving customers and society—thereby fulfilling a purpose instead of merely pursuing an end in itself—become rich sources of meaning and appreciation for their employees. Their employees feel that they are doing some good to somebody or something through the work they perform for their company—in other words, that they are making a meaningful contribution. At the same time, they anticipate the appreciation that goes hand in hand with this. Their potential and willingness to perform are correspondingly high, and this spills over into the company's performance potential—"my goals, your goals, the company's goals are finally one and the same!"(Gertrud Höhler).

The second important reason is that these meaning- and performance-oriented businesses have the awareness of and the motivation and understanding for how they can synergistically combine their services for their customers with a benefit to society. This can result in direct economic benefits along their entire value chain, such as a reduction in transportation and production costs, access to high-quality raw materials, healthier employees, and so on—to name but a few references to sources that give them comparative competitive advantages over companies that place short-term profit maximization above everything else. This idea of a synergistic relationship between business and society relates to the approach of creating shared value developed by Porter/Kramer.

The third main reason why businesses that place themselves first and foremost at the service of their customers and society prosper is that these companies benefit from their excellent reputation in the community. This gives them access to resources that are almost entirely inaccessible for primarily self-serving companies. Their reputation brings them recognition—the best people want to work for them—and in combination with a strong brand, this creates a "positive prejudice" among their customers. The media is sympathetic toward them, and they are often able to build a high degree of trust with lenders, government, and politicians—this, in turn, is their key to economically important resources.

Coevolution—Key to a New Era of Economic Thinking and Business Practice

Coevolution is the maxim of the future, with sustainable promotion of life its guiding star: in the long run, it is not the companies that maximize short-term self-interest that will survive but rather those that believe in serving and empowering their partners in order to experience growth and prosperity together.

The Value Balance in Business as a Tool for Audits and Assessments

The first part of this book deals with developing a reference model for a meaning- and performance-centered enterprise philosophy and culture, as has just been outlined, based on contemporary motivation theory and empirical research. The second part represents a proven tool—the Value

Balance in Business—that enables companies to systematically develop and sustain a meaning- and performance-centered corporate philosophy and culture that is tailored to their needs.

The key questions at the core of a Value Balance in Business corporate culture assessment or audit are as follows:

1. To what extent do employees see meaning in their work?
2. To what extent do they experience recognition as individuals in the company?
3. How pronounced is the resulting motivation on the part of the employees?

The Value Balance in Business uses a structured grid to systematically assess the extent to which employees experience meaning and recognition in the company. Its perspectives derive from a consideration of all the areas in the company where sources of meaning and recognition exist or could exist. These are listed below:

1. Leadership or senior management
2. Mission, vision, and values
3. The relationship between employees and customers
4. The employees themselves and their dispositions
5. The attitude employees have toward the company's products and services
6. The company's market position and capacity for innovation from the employees' point of view
7. The company's reputation in society, as gauged by the employees
8. The shareholders and their attitude toward the company, from the employees' perspective
9. Internal communications, their credibility and usefulness as assessed by the employees
10. Motivation as a dependent variable of the empirical model is defined by three items (formed to an index):
    a. Degree of loyalty that employees have toward the company
    b. Level of motivation toward the company
    c. General personal performance in carrying out professional tasks

This is the basic format for all Value Balance in Business audits and assessments. Data is collected in each of these areas through online surveys or printed questionnaires. With its nine dimensions, the Value Balance in Business audit is clearly much more diverse (i.e., much more nuanced) than most tools of a similar kind. This is in particular due to the inclusion of Perspective 2 (mission, vision, and values), Perspective 3 (customers), Perspective 5 (products and services), Perspective 6 (market position and innovation), and Perspective 8 (shareholders). With this diversity of perspectives, the Value Balance in Business audit embraces a variety of possible sources of meaning and appreciation and provides several different measures for increasing employee motivation. This follows the old physicians' rule that the treatment can only be as good as the diagnosis.

The Role of Creating Shared Value (CSV)

How a company translates a meaningful and performance-centered corporate philosophy and culture into tangible, day-to-day *commercial activity*, however (i.e., how it designs a value-creation process in line with a meaningful and performance-centered corporate philosophy and culture), is a question that Michael E. Porter and Mark R. Kramer address in a way that is very promising for the future of business and the economy with their concept of "creating shared value" (CSV).[1]

The Value Balance in Business embeds the concept of creating shared value in the philosophy and culture of the company, giving it deeper meaning and impact and ensuring that it is practiced permanently and consistently.

---

[1] Michael E. Porter and Mark R. Kramer, "Creating Shared Value: How to Reinvent Capitalism—and Unleash a Wave of Innovation and Growth," *Harvard Business Review* (January–February 2011).

2. New Thinking for a New Era—From Maximizing Short-Term Gain to Coevolution

The idea that profit is a natural by-
product of doing something well, not
an end in itself, is also most universal
(among excellent companies).
    —Thomas J. Peters and Robert H. Waterman

2.1 Creating Shared Value (CSV) as per Porter/Kramer— A Promising Yet Underrated Concept in the Business World

The second Industrial Revolution in the mid-nineteenth century coincided with severe ethical uncertainty within English society. It resulted in the emergence of two utopias at the same time in the same place, both of which would have a lasting impact on world history. The socialist utopia of Karl Marx had well and truly foundered by the late twentieth century, and the utilitarian utopia of John Stuart Mill and Jeremy Bentham has also exceeded its use-by date—the signs of this are unmistakable. The following verdict is a very astute summary and all the more compelling because it does not come from a fundamental business critic but rather a very prominent business professor and advisor of many large companies around the world—Michael E. Porter (together with Mark R. Kramer). In their eyes, the system of capitalism is under siege because, in recent years, business has been viewed as an important source of economic, social, and environmental problems. Their explanation is that companies themselves adhere to an antiquated approach to value creation:

> They continue to view value creation narrowly, optimizing short-term financial performance in a bubble

while missing the most important customer needs and ignoring the broader influences that determine their longer-term success.[2]

In Porter and Kramer's view, the solution lies in the business world's ability to bring business and society back together. The creation of shared value is the key to this process. It involves creating economic value in a way that also produces value for society by taking into account its needs and challenges. Porter and Kramer's credo and ceterum censeo:

> Business must reconnect company success with social progress.

According to Porter/Kramer, companies can organize their business activities in such a way that they combine value creation for the company with similar benefits to society and achieve competitive advantage in the process. Porter/Kramer suggest they do this by:

1. Designing their products appropriately (e.g., through investment in the development of environmental technologies), and defining new markets (such as the introduction of microfinance in the United States)
2. Taking initiatives along the value chain:
   - in energy consumption and logistics (e.g., by reducing transport distances through shrewd purchasing strategies, which will benefit the environment and reduce transport costs)
   - in their use of resources (e.g., by conserving water)
   - in procurement (e.g., by purchasing from local/regional producers and cutting out the middleman and associated speculative elements, thus giving suppliers and customers increased security while raising product quality)
   - in distribution (such as insurance policies via mobile phone in the third world, which reduces the cost to both insured and insurer and eliminates unscrupulous insurance agents)

---

[2] Porter and Kramer, "Creating Shared Value."

- in employee productivity (e.g., through antismoking campaigns that promote the health of employees, saving the company huge health-care costs and reducing absenteeism in the company)
- in location policy (production closer to the sales markets, which in turn reduces transport costs, etc.)
3. Through the development of local business clusters

The Porter/Kramer idea of encouraging companies to exercise their social responsibility by linking appropriate initiatives with profitable business models is as fascinating as it is forward-looking; in many ways, the idea of shared value for the corporate world and society opens up promising future prospects. However, the huge potential identified by Porter and Kramer cannot be fully harnessed for reasons that include the following:

1. Porter/Kramer confine the shared-value approach strictly to the level of corporate conduct and actions: "The concept of shared value can be defined as policies and operating practices that enhance the competitiveness of a company while simultaneously advancing the economic and social conditions in the communities in which it operates."[2] If certain conduct and actions (here: "policies" and "operating practices") are to be sustained over a long period of time within a company, it is necessary to entrench the actions at the higher level of awareness and motivation (philosophy and culture).
2. Porter explicitly supports the pursuit of self-interest as a theory of motivation: "The power of entrepreneurship motivated by self-interest is much stronger than any other force that we can mobilize."[3] This motivation theory impedes the creation of shared value at the expense of businesses and society more than it facilitates it.
3. There are strong interdependencies between corporate structure and organization on the one hand and the effectiveness of the

---

[3] F. Rittmeyer, "Das war kurzfristig gedacht" [That was short-term thinking], *Schweizer Monat* 988 (July/August 2011), 51.

shared-value approach on the other. The issue of corporate structure and organization is not addressed by Porter/Kramer.

These three points are explained in more detail below.

2.1.1 Entrenching the Shared-Value Approach within the Company

For the concept of shared value to have any chance of becoming firmly entrenched or effective in the long term, the appropriate conduct and actions must be anchored in the corporate philosophy and culture (fig. 1). When this is the case, the wider context and purpose becomes clearer to the employees, and their commitment and energy are mobilized. This is the thrust of the Value Balance in Business. It draws on the concept of shared value in the context of a meaning- and performance-centered corporate culture and provides a tool for systematic development and management of that culture.

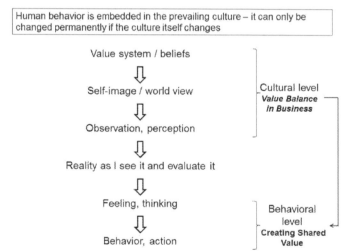

Figure 1. Our value system and our beliefs determine our view of ourselves and our place in the world. They form the "filter" through which we perceive the world and through which we see and evaluate our reality. They are associated with cognitive and emotional processes that guide our behaviors and actions. Change processes that are limited only to the practice of a particular action or behavior are short-lived. Their effects only become permanent when they are embedded in the context of corporate culture—where they have value and meaning.[4]

---

[4] See Heinrich Anker, *Der Sinn im Ganzen* [The meaning of it all]. Münster: ATE Verlag, 2004, 11–20.

2.1.2   On the Motivational Theory of Maximizing Self-Interest

The motivational theory of the pursuit of self-interest is outdated and inefficient; it is based on the paradigm of utilitarianism. This found its way into economic thinking in the mid-nineteenth century and failed to take any account of subsequent advances in many academic disciplines.

One facet of this motivational theory has particularly far-reaching consequences. It was the very assumption that people are driven by a *natural* social instinct[5] that made it possible for the protagonists of utilitarianism—John Stuart Mill and Jeremy Bentham—to formulate the utilitarian paradigm in the middle of the nineteenth century: if people have a *natural* social instinct, they are at their happiest when those closest to them are happiest. Ergo, we contribute to the greatest happiness of the greatest number of people when we strive for our own greatest happiness—or, in terms of the economy, our own greatest benefit.

It did not turn out the way that Mill and Bentham and generations of utilitarian economists had imagined. Utilitarianism and the standard theory of economics, which is based on this concept and is still highly influential today, have fallen far short of their utopia. Wherever the forces of utility maximization have or once had free rein, we have not seen the promised greatest happiness or the greatest benefit to the greatest number but rather human tragedy, economic disaster, a destroyed environment, and any number of other failures—the dioxin disaster in Seveso in 1976, the Bhopal gas tragedy of 1984, the Thalidomide scandal of 1960/61, the Vioxx withdrawal in 2004,[6] the dot.com crisis in

---

[5] "There is this basis of powerful natural sentiment; and this it is which, when once the general happiness is recognized as the ethical standard, will constitute the strength of the utilitarian morality. This firm foundation is that of the social feelings of mankind; the desire to be in unity with our fellow creatures ... tend to become stronger ... from the influence of advancing civilization. The social state is at once so natural, so necessary, and so habitual to man, that ... he never conceives himself otherwise than as a member of a body"—John Stuart Mill, *Utilitarianism*, 5th edition (London: Longmans,1874), 46f.
[6] "Experimental pharmacology had postulated the cardiovascular risk many years ago," said Kay Brune of the University of Erlangen. He was "not really surprised" by the results. Source: Faz.net, 26 July 2011, http://www.faz.net/artikel/C31151/vioxx-skandal-risiken-nebenwirkungen-30072886.html.

2000, the 2008 financial crisis,[7] the European/euro crisis that began in 2010, the Exxon Valdez disaster in Alaska in 1989, Deepwater Horizon in the Gulf of Mexico in 2010, devastating environmental pollution in the oilfields of Nigeria, Enron in 2001, WorldCom in 2002 ... the list goes on. These are just a few examples of the tip of the (rather-too-large) iceberg of unbridled and boundless pursuit of short-term gain in the global economy. These shocking events are occurring more and more frequently and on an increasingly global scale.

When viewed in the light of these consequences of unbridled pursuit of short-term gain, it is difficult to imagine that we are guided by a *natural* social instinct (i.e., with no willful or conscious action on our part). It does not exist, and therefore the paradigm of the greatest benefit for the greatest number as a result of the pursuit of self-interest of all individuals does not lead to the greatest happiness of the greatest number—on the contrary. The commercialization and lack of solidarity inherent in the pursuit of self-interest are doing increasing damage to what were once prosperous economies and functioning societies and are undermining their ability to function. In prosperous economies, the higher the income disparities, the more problems and deficiencies there are in society. Wilkinson and Pickett diagnose the negative consequences of increasing income disparity in the following areas:[8]

- Level of trust
- Mental illness (including drug and alcohol addiction)
- Life expectancy and infant mortality
- Obesity
- Children's educational performance
- Teenage births
- Homicides

---

[7] "Alan Greenspan's 2008 testimony to the US Senate after the collapse of the banking and credit system: 'Those of us who have looked to the self-interest of lending institutions to protect shareholders' equity—myself especially—are in a state of shocked belief,' Greenspan said. 'I've been going for 40 years or more with very considerable evidence that it was working exceptionally well,'" cited in Yochai, "The Unselfish Gene," *Harvard Business Review* (July 2011).

[8] Richard Wilkinson and Kate Pickett, *The Spirit Level: Why Equality Is Better for Everyone* (London: Penguin Books, 2010), 18.

- Imprisonment rates
- Social mobility

These problems do not just affect the victims of the ever-widening income gap—they also impact the more privileged members of these economies and societies.[9] This is impressive empirical evidence that the pursuit of maximum personal benefit does not provide the greatest benefit to the greatest number of people; on the contrary, it decreases it. In the context of maximization of self-interest, the creation of shared value serves more as a damage-limitation measure rather than ushering in a powerful new era in the relationship between business and society.

2.1.3 The Effectiveness of the Shared-Value Approach Depends on Corporate Structures

The structures and organization of companies and corporate performance vary considerably, depending on whether employees are assumed to be driven primarily by the desire to maximize their own self-interest or are capable of acting with freedom and responsibility. The first scenario tends to apply to centralized, very hierarchical, rather inflexible, and not very adaptable command-and-control structures based on distrust, and the second to less hierarchical companies where competencies are located in the best places to meet the needs of their customers. These are better conditions for the successful implementation and effectiveness of the shared-value model than a rigid, centralized, command-and-control structure.

Where the worldview and self-image are based on the motivational theory of maximizing self-interest, corporate vision is directed inward. The focus is on its own needs, and any understanding of the external effects of its activities or their impact on customers, suppliers, and third parties is limited. This is exacerbated by the fact that the utilitarian standard theory of economics mercilessly pillories everything but the pursuit of short-term maximum profit as to the antithesis of successful entrepreneurship. It is a poor starting point for ensuring

---

[9] Ibid., 175–181.

that the shared-value approach is properly accepted by a company and consistently applied with any prospect of success.

Take away: In summary, it can be stated that in the first place, the paradigm of maximizing self-interest has a negative impact on the acceptance of the shared-value approach within the company. Secondly, the structures of such companies rarely offer a suitable basis for optimal implementation of the concept, and thirdly, the structures of such companies and the low level of acceptance also curb enthusiasm within the company for the shared-value concept rather than stimulate any added motivation.

In contrast, the Value Balance in Business offers a contemporary motivation theory. Many human and corporate resources, which are otherwise wasted when the Porter approach of maximizing self-interest is taken, can be mobilized on this basis. When embedded in the context of a meaningful and performance-centered corporate culture, as per the Value Balance in Business model, the shared-value approach can reach new heights and become what Porter and Kramer envisaged: "the next new transformation of business thinking."[1]

Motivation theories and concepts of humanity are of great importance to a company's functional efficiency, adaptability, and long-term viability. In the next three chapters, we will take an in-depth look at this.

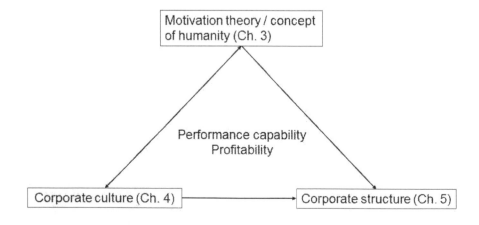

2.2   Successful Entrepreneurship beyond Maximization of Self-Interest

There are basically two ways to respond to the above and many other critical objections to the current standard theory of economics with its motivational theory of maximizing self-interest:

Option 1: Advocates of the utilitarian economic paradigm attempt to justify their stance by arguing that the results of their approach would look a lot more positive if market forces could only operate without hindrance according to their own (i.e., self-serving) laws.[10] A prominent exponent of this argument is Milton Friedman, who opposes everything but corporate maximization of self-interest:

> ... in a free society ... there is one and only one social responsibility of business – to use its resources and engage in activities designed to increase its profits so long as it stays within the rules of the game, which is to say, engages in open and free competition without deception or fraud.[11]

Option 2: Adhere to empiricism and accept that it is possible for responsible companies—who, in the long run, are economically highly successful for this very reason—to exist beyond the primacy of self-interest, meaning short-term maximization of profits or a "fast buck" mentality.

This is supported by several in-depth and well-known studies from the United States that address the correlation between corporate culture and corporate performance. In terms of their research design, these

---

[10] This line of argument is not unlike that of erstwhile representatives of socialism. When it became clearer their utopia was failing, they tried to salvage it by making a distinction between ideal socialism and real (existing) socialism. Even if in reality not everything functions as planned, this in itself is no proof that socialism has failed—only that conditions are not ideal. Similarly, advocates of the standard utilitarian theory of economics regularly point to politics, with its supposedly market-distorting decisions, as the scapegoat for the failure of their economic utopia.

[11] Milton Friedman, "The Social Responsibility of Business Is to Increase Its Profits," *New York Times Magazine* (September 13, 1970): 32–33, 122, 124, 126.

can be arranged in a chronological sequence, with each study seen as a continuation of the preceding one. The series is as follows:

- Peters, Thomas J., and Waterman, Robert H. *In Search of Excellence: Lessons from America's Best Run Companies.* New York: Harper & Row, 1982.
- Kotter, John P., and Heskett, James L. *Corporate Culture and Performance.* New York: The Free Press, 1992.
- Collins, James C., and Porras, Jerry I. *Built to Last: Successful Habits of Visionary Companies.* New York: Harper Business Essentials, 2002 (1994).
- Joyce, W., Nohria, N., and Roberson, B. *What (Really) Works: The 4+2 Formula for Sustained Business Success.* New York: Harper Business, 2003.

These studies all have one thing in common. In the long run,[12] companies are particularly robust and highly profitable when:

1. they look beyond their own interests, (i.e., when they allow themselves to be guided by the primacy of performance and not by the maximization of short-term gain or shareholder value as an end in itself). In all these studies, customers act as the recipients of service; in Kotter/Heskett we also encounter employees and shareholders as stakeholder groups, and in Collins/Porras in many cases even society.
2. they show their appreciation of their employees, regard them as individuals, and make it possible for them to contribute as individuals to their work.

---

[12] The observation periods vary according to the number of years: ten (Joyce, Nohria, Roberson), eleven (Kotter/Heskett), twenty (Peters/Waterman), and sixty-four years (Collins/Porras). Companies with a performance-centric corporate culture obviously have high life expectancy.

> From a business perspective, one fact is particularly interesting. Depending on the study and key indicator (e.g., Total Return to Shareholders or Growth of Stock Prices), the long-term revenues of companies guided by the primacy of performance and respectful interaction with their employees exceed those of companies acting on the self-serving primacy of profit or maximization of shareholder value—by six to nine times.[13]

There are good reasons for this. We will see that a company's performance primacy and its appreciation of its employees' ability and willingness to perform are of fundamental importance—and thus in various respects greatly enhance corporate performance.[14] The performance primacy, moreover, provides the company with that which are also of economic value to the company; they offer the company comparative advantages over companies acting on the primacy of short-term gain.

Placing the interests of customers and society as well as respectful treatment of employees first is the antithesis of the Darwinian model of "survival of the fittest," which is based purely on self-interest.

- A self-serving company does not side with its customers but approaches them as opposites or even adversaries. It seeks the fastest way to squeeze the maximum out of them in exchange for the minimum amount of effort. The same attitude is applied to its employees, suppliers, local communities, use of resources

---

[13] See John P. Kotter and James L. Heskett, *Corporate Culture and Performance* (New York: The Free Press, 1992), 11; James C. Collins and Jerry I. Porras, *Built to Last: Successful Habits of Visionary Companies*, (New York: Harper Business Essentials, 2002), 5; William Joyce, Nitin Nohria, and Bruce Roberson, *What (Really) Works: The 4+2 Formula for Sustained Business Success* (New York: Harper Business, 2003), 14f. *In Search of Excellence* focused on a sample of financially successful companies in the respective sector; in this study, unlike the next one, no direct comparison between successful and less successful companies is drawn.

[14] The ability to perform applies when employees are not hampered in their performance by psychological barriers or stress generated by their working environment; the willingness to perform refers to the exercise of free will to provide a service in and for the company—and any other recipients. Together, that ability and willingness to perform add up to performance delivery, and this is measured empirically.

(such as water, air, and soil), and removal of environmentally harmful by-products or waste.

- When the aim is to maximize short-term gains or increase market share, it may be more useful—that is to say, more profitable—for companies to wage war on their competitors directly by, for instance, stifling their resources rather than outperforming them in the market. Failing this, it may be even cheaper for companies to cooperate with their competitors through price fixing or cartels at the expense of their customers.
- In these circumstances, it is not always the best product or the best service that prevails.

Self-interested companies are increasingly guilty of raiding their economic, social, and natural environment, and in so doing depleting their own resources. However, in the long run, the fittest are not the "self-servers" who fatten themselves at the expense of others and deprive them of their resources in the process but rather those who maintain an awareness of the common good while adapting quickly and efficiently to changing conditions. Symbiosis and synergy are the way forward. They make those involved in the system stronger, with everybody benefiting from everybody else.

- The customers benefit from companies that solve their problems effectively and efficiently and thus enhance their potential for performance; the companies in return benefit from productive, dynamic customers.
- The companies benefit from employees who are willing to give their best because they are treated with dignity; the employees themselves benefit from companies that enable them to use their skills fully and perform meaningful work, paying them good wages thanks to sustained economic success.
- The suppliers take advantage from companies that do not squeeze them dry but instead leave them with the resources they need for their own development; and companies gain from suppliers who are up to date and absolutely first class in terms of their technology, quality, innovation capacity, and delivery performance.

- Shareholders receive an advantage from prospering companies, and these companies in return gain from shareholders who have an interest in long-term prosperity for the company.
- Other important symbioses and synergies include those between companies and local communities, between companies and society, and also between companies and the environment.

In the long run, systems in which the players—consumers, businesses, employees, suppliers, shareholders, local communities, and the like—do not focus on the question, how can I get the most out of it for me in the shortest possible time, but instead ask themselves, how can I best serve and support my partners in this interaction, for them also to prosper and thrive to everybody's benefit? Guided by such an evolution, all parties involved have the opportunity to grow, develop, and, in turn, make their partner stronger. In doing so, they themselves become stronger too. Coevolution is the antithesis of the maximization of self-interest. There is no need for business to be a war—it can be of service to everybody!

From a great many insights from various disciplines within science and philosophy, it is becoming increasingly clear that man's evolutionary development cannot primarily be explained and understood through the motivation theory of maximization of self-interest. In contrast to all other species, we humans are highly unspecialized. We do not possess any particularly great physical powers, we are not particularly fast, we have no specific physical attributes for catching prey or self-defense, we are not very resistant to heat or cold, and we are not specialized in any particular milieu. But we do possess powers of understanding and thus a capacity for cooperation and exchange like no other living being. These abilities alone made it possible for us as humans to work together and achieve goals that we would otherwise never have been able to attain as individuals; only because of these human characteristics were we able to unlock all regions of the world, from the Arctic to the Antarctic and even beyond into space, accumulating experience and knowledge—and the scope is growing exponentially. Man's fundamental characteristics are the qualities of exchange and cooperation—not an urge toward self-interest. We will be taking a closer look at this later.

The idea of coevolution has yet another completely different dimension. As *Homo faber*—"man the creator"—man intervenes more and more actively and with greater effect in evolution, changing and shaping the world (our common world) ourselves in ever-greater measure, and this has an increasingly significant effect on us. Today, our evolution as human beings is directly connected to the concept of cocreation. The choice between being guided in the act of cocreation by a spirit of maximizing self-interest or a spirit of coevolution, symbiosis and synergy will prove crucial for our collective future. In this sense, coevolution translates into sustainable promotion of life.

2.3 Successful Protagonists of Socially Responsible Entrepreneurship

The idea of coevolution is not merely utopian wishful thinking. Coevolution is being put into practice; it is merely that—under the normative pressure of the standard theory of economics with its dogma of maximizing self-interest—this idea has not yet taken root in the public consciousness—despite numerous broad and in-depth research studies. To illustrate, let us look at two examples of the application of the philosophy of coevolution from the authoritative source of successful entrepreneurs:

> Because ... multibillion-dollar corporations control vast resources around the globe, employ millions of people, and create and own incredible wealth, they hold the future of the planet in their hands. (...) If corporations run their businesses with the sole aim of gaining more market share or earning more profits, they may well lead the world into economic, environmental and social ruin ... It is our obligation as business leaders to join together to build a foundation for world peace and prosperity.[15]
>
> —Ryuzaburo Kaku, president of
> Canon Inc. 1977–1989, in 1977

---

[15] Ryuzaburo Kaku, "The Path of Kyosei," *Harvard Business Review* 75 (July–August 1997), 62.

I want to discuss <u>why</u> [emphasis by the author] a company exists in the first place. In other words, why are we here? I think many people assume, wrongly, that a company exists simply to make money. While this is an important result of a company's existence, we have to go deeper and find the real reasons for our being. As we investigate this, we inevitably come to the conclusion that a group of people get together and exist as an institution that we call a company so they are able to accomplish something collectively that they could not accomplish separately—they make a contribution to society, a phrase which sounds trite but is fundamental ... You can look around ... and still see people who are interested in money and nothing else, but the underlying drives come largely from a desire to do something else—to make a product—to give a service—generally to do something which is of value.[16]

—David Packard, cofounder of HP, 1960

This understanding of business and entrepreneurship can be generalized. Just like the concept of consistent maximization of self-interest, the philosophy of coevolution also has its protagonists in management theory. The most famous among them is Peter Drucker. As he says:

Business enterprises—and public service institutions as well—are organs of society. They do not exist for their own sake, but to fulfill a specific social purpose and to satisfy a specific need of a society, a community, or individuals. They are not ends in themselves, but means.[17]

---

[16] David Packard, speech given to HP's training group on March 8, 1960, courtesy of Hewlett-Packard Company archives, cited as per Collins and Porras, *Built to Last*, 58, 310.

[17] Peter Drucker, *The Essential Drucker: Selections from the Management Works of Peter F. Drucker*, The Classic Drucker Collection (Amsterdam etc.: Butterworth-Heinemann, 2007), 11.

According to Peter Drucker, companies do not serve an end in itself, such as short-term profit maximization, for example. Instead, they contribute toward fulfilling a particular role in society while meeting the needs of a specific client group—whether this is a society, a community, or individuals. And in turn, businesses derive their meaning, the reason for their existence, from serving their customers and society. Legitimization through performance is the key to those resources that a company needs for long-term prosperity (see fig. 2).

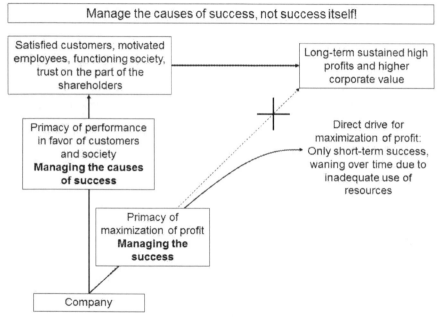

Figure 2. William E. Deming's recommendation for quality management evidently also ensures high profitability and corporate value for the company in the long run: "Manage the causes, not the results!"

To summarize, companies achieve well-above-average long-term success when they look beyond themselves and consistently maintain their external orientation, meaning:

1. when they place themselves at the service of their customers
2. when they place themselves at the service of society—which also includes the natural environment as the basis for the life of any society

3. when they treat their employees with appreciation and not merely as yet another resource

These three approaches form a good basis for creating shared value. This in turn enhances the performance of these companies for the benefit of society. As we shall see in chapter 4, benefits aimed at society also have a positive impact on the motivation of a company's employees. In this context, creating shared value not only brings the company economic benefits directly but also indirectly in the form of employee motivation.

Under these circumstances, companies become real "service entities," and they have a "face." In other words, they are distinctive, and through their services, they become indispensable to their customers and society. This could well be the best life insurance policy.

These companies that follow an approach of coevolution are in a synergistic, ultimately balanced relationship of sharing resources with their environment—most notably their customers, employees, market, society, the environment, and shareholders. This process of growing together requires time, which is why these companies are not focused on maximizing and dressing up the next quarter's profit. They think and act in much longer time frames, allowing them to grow synergistically while at the same time distancing themselves from the things that do not support this approach.

The long-term elevated returns of primarily performance-based and employee-friendly companies could be interpreted as a return on investment—in other words, a return on the long-term development of certain types of capital and the associated increase in productivity.

It is in particular the creation and accumulation of

- Trust in the company
  - among the employees themselves and between employees and managers

- on the part of customers (one indication of this is the power of the company's brand) and society (the company's reputation) as the recipients of the company's services
- from shareholders, lenders, suppliers, government authorities, and politicians

• The employees' gift of spirit—creativity ability, and willingness for innovation; willingness to cooperate; constructive crisis and conflict management; an attitude of serving a greater whole (society, community, business) and serving other people (customers, team members, supervisors or employees, etc.); freedom to assume responsibility; intrinsic motivation

• Knowledge capital—this can begin as intellectual capital and grow from there, provided that the treatment of employees is not guided by short-term cost calculations and a hire-and-fire approach and that there is good internal communication in all directions

These are all characteristics of a performance-oriented corporate culture. They also have a positive impact on the effectiveness and efficiency of the company's processes and structures.

These types of capital are all based on people and are in direct relation to respectful interaction with employees.

Companies who pursue short-term profit maximization are not in a position to keep up in this regard, because cultures that focus on maximizing self-interest are cultures of mutual mistrust determined by command-and-control structures. They make it impossible to allow employees to apply their primal human abilities, such as cooperation, creativity, innovation, freedom, and responsibility, with corresponding negative consequences for both the employees and the company. This is also no foundation upon which to create effective and efficient shared value.

2.4 Garbage Collecting or Coevolution? We Hold the Fate of Humanity in Our Hands

We have already mentioned briefly that as creative beings, we are not passively subjected to evolution—we stand in relation to it through cocreation and coevolution. Wherever and however we intervene in our increasingly globalized world, it has its effects on us and, whether we like it or not, is increasingly transforming us into a community that shares a common destiny: tomorrow and beyond, we and/or our children and grandchildren will inevitably have to reap what we sow today.

We are currently standing at a crossroads. We can continue as before—in other words, we can carry on in our pursuit of maximum self-interest. However, the price is high. Evolutionary biologist Gerhard Neuweiler writes: "In an unbridled frenzy for power and through unrestrained individual greed for money and might, we have created an exploitative consumerist society that has spread throughout the world. Based on a monetary hierarchy which is capable of destroying humanity's future, it is turning human societies into garbage dumps for products, and human beings into garbage disposal units."[18]

Or we could let ourselves be guided by the concept of coevolution, as Piero Ferrucci puts it:

> It may sound strange and paradoxical, but it is true that the most sensible way to promote one's own interests, gain one's own freedom and find one's own happiness is often not by pursuing these goals directly, but by being aware of other people's interests, alleviating their fears and sorrows and contributing to their happiness. It's all really very simple. You don't have to choose between being kind to yourself and others. It's one and the same.[19]

---

[18] Gerhard Neuweiler, *Und wir sind es doch—die Krone der Evolution* [We are it—the crown of evolution] (Berlin: Wagenbach, 2009), 228.

[19] Piero Ferrucci, *Nur die Freundlichen überleben. Warum wir lernen müssen, mit dem Herzen zu denken, wenn wir eine Zukunft haben wollen* [The power of kindness: the unexpected benefits of leading a compassionate life], 1st edition (Berlin: Ullstein, 2006), 246.

The decision to either favor maximization of self-interest or take a coevolution approach is not something that contains a host of unknowns; it is not a decision riddled with uncertainty. We have already shown that the concept of coevolution is in many ways economically superior to that of the maximization of self-interest and that business does not have to mean war. This is demonstrated by numerous entrepreneurs and their actual experiences, as well as through studies such as those of Peters/Waterman (*In Search of Excellence*), Kotter/Heskett (*Corporate Culture and Performance*), Collins/Porras (*Built to Last: Successful Habits of Visionary Companies*), and Joyce/Nohria/Roberson (*What Really Works: The 4+2 Formula for Sustained Business Success*), to name but a few.

2.5 Why Performance-Oriented Companies Are More Successful— In Search of Humanity

We now know that a culture of external orientation, an approach focusing on the primacy of performance, and the respectful treatment of human beings *does* bestow companies with benefits in the long run. In this book, we examine *why* this is the case. Only once we understand this will it become possible to selectively align the culture with the company's capacity for performance in terms of coevolution. In doing so, we place the spotlight on the employees. With their motivation, with their ability and willingness to perform, they are ultimately the "engine" of the whole system—they are the source of moral capital and the bearers of intellectual and knowledge capital, and the productive application of these is dependent on them. In short:

> An increase in the value of a company begins with an increase in appreciation for its employees.

We will see that, together with an appreciation for people, performance primacy and coevolution are fundamental human needs. When these needs are met, they act as catalysts of employees' capacity and willingness for performance.

3. Mankind's Spiritual Capital—A Unique Asset That Transcends Self-Interest

Enthusiasm is the mother of effort, and
without it nothing great was ever achieved.
—Ralph Waldo Emerson

3.1 No Other Resources Are as Valuable as Human Resources, and None Are So Recklessly Squandered

The more people feel at home in a society, in a community or a relationship, in an institution, or in an organization, the more likely they are to be mentally willing and able to contribute their full range of skills and apply all their strength to jointly create something which alone they would not have been capable of, as David Packard put it (see chapter 2.3)—and the more robust and stable the corresponding social structures will be.[20] This raises the question that is central to this chapter: under what conditions do people feel so at home in a business and at the same time so authentic as an individual that they are willing and able to give their best? It is a question that leads us back to the concepts of humanity and motivation theory and ultimately to yet other questions. What lies at the heart of the human being? What are our basic needs? What forms the

---

[20] This applies to social entities of all sizes: people literally drove away from the system of socialism in 1989 or—as was the case in Berlin—ran away; today, social subsystems are experiencing stages of disintegration in many countries, such as the Catholic and Evangelical Churches in Europe, which are losing members; the national defense force, which is faced in many places with a declining combat spirit; the unions, which have for many years been losing members; and the political system, in which parties are increasingly confronted with floating voters and which in many places has lost the trust of the people entirely. This disintegration is also reflected in the microcosm of marriage, as more and more marriages are ending in divorce—and the list goes on.

hearth for our inner fire? What is the spark that sets it alight? What can a company do to fuel this fire?

In today's self-serving corporate world and its narrow scope on maximizing short-term shareholder value, this flame is but a flicker; incredible potential is left to lie idly. No other resources are nearly as valuable as human resources—it is people with their ideas, their creativity, their will to make even better that which is already good, to push the boundaries ever further, who ultimately keep things going and create growth and development in society, culture, and the economy. Yet it seems that no other resource is squandered to quite the same degree. The following are just a few pointers to demonstrate the extent to which many employees currently lack any feeling of being at home or being authentically individual in their work and with their employer:

- According to the 2010 Gallup Engagement Index, 70–90 percent of all employees in the major national economies had only a weak or no relationship with their work and their employer[21]— not even a relationship based on criticism, which would still mean that they have at least an interest in matters concerning the company and their own work.
- Worldwide, around 50 percent of all employees would be willing to make concessions concerning their wages or their professional status in exchange for doing more meaningful work.[22]
- Even in countries with a relatively high engagement index, such as Switzerland, the largest shortcoming is in the appreciation shown to employees. In surveys conducted in 1979, 1994, and 2003, the results regularly indicated that 52–53 percent of young employees wanted more recognition, and these figures are representative of a large number of comparable studies. Nowhere else—not even in the areas of job structuring, remuneration,

---

[21] Source: Engagement Index—International Comparison 2010, "The State of the Global Workplace," Gallup 2010.

[22] The question was "Would you take on a lesser role or lower wage if you felt that your work contributed to something more important or meaningful to you or your organization?" Source: Kelly Services, media release "Around the Globe the Desire for Meaningful Work Triumphs Over Pay, Promotion, and Job Choices" (Troy, MI: February 25, 2009).

staff development, or job security—did employees indicate shortcomings that are similarly significant.[23]

- In Europe, North America, and Asia, 80–90 percent of all employees expressed a preference for employers who act in ethically and socially responsible ways and who are considered to be environmentally friendly.[24] Against the background of the state of play in the economic and corporate world, here too there is a significant rift between employees and the world of business and the corporation, as Michael Porter points out in chapter 2.1.

- "Scientific management" in the tradition of Taylor leads to increasing alienation between people and their work. Henry Mintzberg refers to this approach and the consequences it has for people and companies: "Thus has the cult of rationality, as manifested in so-called professional management, served to destroy the deep-rooted effectiveness of many of our large organizations, by squeezing out their very humanness. In its own form of reduction to absurdity, professional management made organizations so rational, so efficient, that they ceased to function effectively."[25]

The less we see our work as an opportunity to become actively and responsibly involved in shaping our world—which is, after all, our home—the more alienated we become. We become more and more estranged from other people and ultimately from ourselves, and this quenches whatever inner fire we have, whatever joy we find in our own abilities and the chance to work together with others toward something which, on our own, we are not capable of achieving. This effectively turns a person into someone who is only preoccupied with him- or herself, who is only concerned with maximizing his or her own self-interest, a rootless and homeless creature that we could call the *"Homo*

---

[23] Ruth Meyer Schweizer, Karl W. Haltiner, and Luca Bertossa, *Werte und Lebenschancen im Wandel. Eine Studie zu den Lebens-, Bildungs-, Arbeits- und Politkorientierungen junger Erwachsener in der Schweiz* [Values and life opportunities in transition: a trend study on the orientation of young adults in switzerland toward life, education, employment and politics], Academic series, (Zurich/Chur: Rüegger, 2008), 165.

[24] Source: Kelly Services, media release "Social responsibility key to attracting top talent" (Troy, MI: October 28, 2009).

[25] Henry Mintzberg, *Inside our Strange World of Organizations* (New York: The Free Press, 1989), 351.

economicus"—exactly the view that the standard utilitarian theory of economics has of the "human being." It is in the interest of people as well as companies that this concept of humanity is finally replaced by a modern motivation theory.

3.2 That Special Human Touch

Right up to Sigmund Freud, Herbert Spencer, and Frederick Winslow Taylor, the nineteenth century was inspired by the belief that human life and coexistence can be explained and shaped through means of quasi-scientific laws. Freud's motivation theory shows striking analogies with thermodynamics (the individual as a bundle of instincts, which, when the pressure becomes too great, causes the "boiler" to explode). Herbert Spencer, by transposing Darwin's theory of natural selection to human society, became the pioneer of social Darwinism—survival of the fittest and the pursuit of self-interest are legitimized as requirements for survival and the superiority of societies. This was fertile soil for Taylor to establish his "scientific management," as noted in the quotation from Mintzberg: it is a synthesis of the nineteenth-century, self-serving concept of humanity and the rampant technological euphoria of the same era. The concept of "scientific management" also gave rise to Taylor's social loafing hypothesis. This theory postulates that employees willingly hold back on their performance in order to maximize their own benefits. What it means is that management must be familiar with every work task and step in the work process, in the greatest detail, and then also manage the company as if it were a big machine—only once this is achieved can there be transparency and controllability, thus making it impossible for employees to loaf by holding back on their performance.

In contrast to this and to its credit, early in the twentieth century, philosophical anthropology identified mankind's special position in relation to nature. The best-known names connected with this school of thought are those of the philosophers Max Scheler, Helmuth Plessner, Arnold Gehlen, and, with regard to certain aspects, also Odo Marquard. In the form of meaning-centered psychology, Viktor Frankl (1905– 1997) in particular made philosophical anthropology a fruitful field for psychology, molding it into a motivation theory in its own right. (He can be viewed, with some justification, as the real founder of Positive Psychology.)

3.2.1 The Human Being—Receptive to the World

In philosophical anthropology's concept of humanity, we—just like all other living things—also have reflexes driven by instincts and urges and impulses rooted in the psyche (see fig. 3). But in human beings, they do not unfurl to their full extent; we are not entirely determined by them. As human beings, we are more than the sum of our natural abilities— that is to say, more than just our instincts and psyche.

In the sense of philosophical anthropology, it can be stated that mankind is indeed *of* nature but is *not ruled by nature alone*. The human being's manifestation of nature—that is to say, our instincts and psychological impulses—do not fully envelop and control us.[26] We are able to look beyond our urges and instincts and see ourselves and the world.[27] It is not nature but culture that constitutes our very own world as humans, a world that belongs exclusively to mankind—the world of symbols, values, and meaning, of norms and beliefs, aesthetics, knowledge, communication, and comprehension.[28]

This degree of freedom with regard to nature is what philosophical anthropology calls mankind's spiritual dimension—this is what distinguishes us from all other beings. It is a very pragmatic notion of the human spirit, defined by the ability we humans have to distance ourselves by our self-awareness and our capacity for self-transcendence. These are attributes that can be observed empirically.

---

[26] This has now empirically been confirmed by neurobiology: "The ability to control our immediate feelings and make them subordinate to long-term goals through 'cool deliberation' is what distinguishes humans from the entire animal kingdom." See Neuweiler, *Und wir sind es doch*, 184.

[27] In this context, philosophical anthropology often refers to the human being as not a creature defined by nature but one that looks beyond nature, a self-defining being.

[28] All these aspects of culture point to the existence of an *other*—in the world of culture, the human being as an individual is never alone.

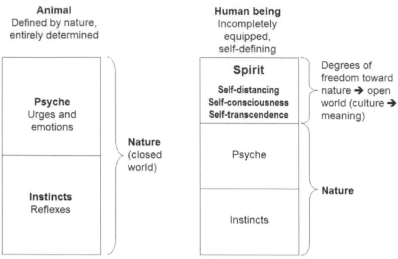

Philosophical anthropology's concept of humanity (Max Scheler, Helmut Plessner, Arnold Gehlen, Odo Marquard)

Figure 3. As human beings, we have a degree of freedom when it comes to our nature—what distinguishes us from animals is that we are incompletely equipped in terms of physical reflexes and psychological impulses. Philosophical anthropology thus describes the human being as something of an "imperfect being"—whether this can indeed be considered a shortcoming may be worthy of debate.

3.2.2 Self-Distancing: We Have the Capacity to Take a Step Back from Our Self-Serving Instincts and Urges

Because we have a degree of freedom from our own natural character, we are always in a position to recognize the instinctive feelings (reflexes) originating from our physical being and the emotional impulses (psyche) for what they are; we can objectify them and step outside of them—and *in principle* willingly face them or possibly even confront them (see fig. 4). One indication of this is that we can talk about our feelings and thoughts, and another is that we are not compelled to obey stimulus-response mechanisms. For example, we do not have to respond to a malicious e-mail instinctively (as if forced) by reacting in the same tone. We can leave it be for a while, distance ourselves and our emotions from it by letting time pass, and then act later when we have given it some thought—whether by answering in a considered manner or deliberately refraining from answering.

Although we are not always successful in distancing ourselves like this,[29] the fact remains that there is real potential to do so. But *Homo economicus*, preoccupied only with self-interest (the concept of humanity that the self-serving standard theory of economics adheres to), does not have this ability. In pursuit only of happiness and personal benefit, these beings are always at the center of their own world. Unable to distance themselves from this world, they are caught in the vice of nature just like the plants and the animals, remaining mere slaves to their instincts and psychological impulses.

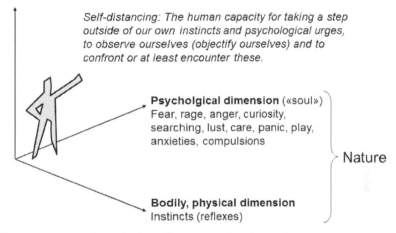

The dimensions of humanity in philosophical anthropology and meaning-centered psychology

Dimension of spirit

Self-distancing: The human capacity for taking a step outside of our own instincts and psychological urges, to observe ourselves (objectify ourselves) and to confront or at least encounter these.

Psycholgical dimension («soul»)
Fear, rage, anger, curiosity, searching, lust, care, panic, play, anxieties, compulsions

Nature

Bodily, physical dimension
Instincts (reflexes)

Figure 4. Body, mind, and spirit—the three dimensions of the human being.

According to meaning-centered psychology, our capacity for *distancing ourselves*[30] is not just restricted to our internal environment (physical and psychological impulses and urges) but also extends to the pressure

---

[29] We have expressions that refer to this; we can be "blinded by love" or "blinded by hatred"; the reference to ourselves can be so strong that we, like Narcissus, become victims of ourselves.

[30] Their physical origins have now been discovered: it is the dorsal medial prefrontal cortex (dMPFC). This area has a veto function over possible activities, including those that may already have been prepared in the subconscious. The dMPFC is one of the most important players in self-control and is a faculty of mankind that sets us apart from the animal world. See Neuweiler, *Und wir sind es doch*, 180.

of expectation and the herd instinct of our external, social environment. People respond to the expectations directly placed on them as well as societal values, norms, customs, traditions, and rituals and can choose to accept these or willfully reject them. For instance, when given a task, we almost involuntarily ask ourselves, *Why? What for?* or *For whom?* We evaluate or distance ourselves, and only then do we make a decision. To put it another way, anyone who wants to stand out in the market must be able to swim against the tide, if needs be. This is Sam Walton's legendary maxim: "Swim upstream. Go the other way. Ignore the conventional wisdom …!"[31]

The philosopher Peter Bieri also touches on our capacity for detachment from our instincts and our urges: "We have the ability to create an inner distance from our thoughts, feelings and desires, and to test and evaluate them."[32]

What this means is that, in contrast to the utilitarian concept of humanity, we humans have free will. Herein lies the core of our individual freedom and responsibility. This in turn has far-reaching consequences for people management as well as companies' structures and organization and their functionality or performance.

3.2.3   The Fully Capable Human Being Has the Other in Mind Besides the Self

As beings capable of taking a step back from ourselves, we humans do not merely think, feel, and act but have the potential to be aware *that* we think and *what* we think, feel, and do. We perceive ourselves as a feeling, thinking, and acting subject; we develop self-identity, and we are *self-conscious*. *Homo economicus*, on the other hand, preoccupied as it is with its own instincts and urges, does not have this ability.

The moment that we perceive ourselves as a defined "self," we must inevitably also become aware of the existence of the "other." Without an

---

[31] Wal-Mart founder Sam Walton.
[32] Peter Bieri,"Was heisst es, über unser Leben selbst zu bestimmen?" [What does it mean to determine our own lives?], *ZEIT Magazine* 24 (July 2007): 49.

other, without the "you" from whom I can and must distinguish myself, there can be no coherent, distinguished self. When we enter the world, this other—this *you*—initially consists of our closest reference figures. Soon, however, a wider sphere of people becomes visible, and it is through them that culture is mediated for us in the form of language, norms, and societal values. We cannot escape encounters with this other—it is a primal experience that probably has its origins in the womb.

What we are dealing with here is unity/wholeness based on a dichotomy: in order to maintain our self-identity, we human beings must differentiate ourselves from the other, from the *you*—and yet, for this very reason, we must always remain in a relationship with the other/*you*. Karl Jaspers put it very succinctly: "When I am entirely myself, I am not merely myself."[33]

This brings us to *our first fundamental human need:* that of *recognition by the you by other people.* This is vitally important to us as humans. Without this encounter, we cannot develop a stable self-identity; without this encounter, it is not possible for us to perceive ourselves in a broad sense as a unique, *coherent* self, as subject.

A stable, unique, and distinctive self cannot evolve if the self considers him- or herself as an absolute—that is to say, if he or she separates him- or herself from all their references as *Homo economicus* does, caught up in itself and its self-interests. Then again, a stable self cannot evolve if I lose myself completely in the other/*you* but only in interaction with the other, the *you*.[34]

---

[33] Where this is not the case, our self-identity is threatened; for example, this may happen when people become victims of bullying. In the sense that the victim of bullying is denied recognition as a person, this constitutes a kind of "social murder." Our self-identity is also at risk when we constantly silence the impartial "inner audience" of Adam Smith's ethical conscience and refuse to consider ourselves from the perspective of others and understand the consequences of our actions from their perspective.

[34] This does not so much concern the balance between altruism and egotism but the balance between self/*I* and other. Sometimes when the self separates from the other, it is not a sign of selfishness but a question of protecting the self; it is self-assertion, the preservation of one's own identity. *Homo economicus* is, however, a stranger to this dimension of balancing between self and other; it only functions at the level of egotism-altruism, because it has no identity.

This has us far removed from mankind's *natural* social instinct,[5] which functions without free will, as postulated by John Stuart Mill. Maintaining our identity is much rather a continuous balancing act between the self/*I* and the other/*you*. We are aided in this by the human capacity for empathy, the ability to put ourselves in another person's shoes and see the world from his or her perspective. It allows us to understand and assess the impact we have on the other. It is thanks to our capacity for empathy and for distancing ourselves that we are always at once both subject and object; we are both the "perpetrators" and "victims" of our actions—we can and must maintain a balance.[35]

Our final guiding force, however, is our ethical conscience. And yet our capacity for distancing ourselves is nevertheless such that we are able to break free from the voice of our ethical conscience—we have the freedom and the responsibility to choose whether we respond to it or not. Our *Homo economicus* of the utilitarian standard theory of economics does not have the same concern for striking a balance—it has neither self-consciousness nor the capacity for empathy or an ethical conscience.

Time and again, when I am in conversation with employees and managers, I experience just how paralyzing people of flesh and blood find this unscrupulousness and lack of empathy that mainstream economics accepts so willfully. Many people are torn by the conflict between the (erroneous) belief that maximizing self-interest is the only way to economic success and the voice of their conscience, which requires of them something other than short-term maximization of profit by all available means.[11] Some find the courage to swim against the tide; others become depressed, burn out, suffer a heart attack, or try to deal with their conflicts by resorting to medication or drugs—and in the most tragic cases, even contemplate suicide.[36]

---

[35] Adam Smith postulated this in his first revolutionary work *The Theory of Moral Sentiments*, in 1759.

[36] According to the *Economist*, the US Bureau of Labor Statistics determined that the number of suicides related to professional work increased by 28 percent from 2007 to 2008—and this rate is still lower than in Europe. The *Economist* further reports that suicide is just the tip of work-related frustration. Source: "Hating What You Do," *Economist* (October 8, 2009).

It might be argued that conscience is not a scientific field, that it cannot be precisely defined, much less weighed and measured. While this is true, it is a fact that conscience remains an experience felt by a great many if not most people;[37] there are countless testimonies to this. Furthermore, it cannot be denied that conscience has a significant influence on our actions—especially in exchange and management relations, which are indeed at the core of the economic sciences. (In his *The Theory of Moral Sentiments*, Adam Smith referred to the effectiveness of the human conscience.) This is one reason why various training facilities teach ethics and examine case studies that raise ethical questions. However, as long as such training remains limited to case studies without the formation of conscience (a key aspect of people's spiritual capital) it will not lead to ethical business behavior.

Mankind's capacity for empathy and for stepping outside the self is of the highest significance for a company's long-term economic success:

> Only by using this human ability to step outside ourselves and thereby turn our gaze away from ourselves, from our own instincts and urges and to look beyond ourselves, can we really encounter other people and they us. It is only on the basis of mutual empathy that we are capable of truly understanding each other, of building trust and using this as a foundation from which to cooperate toward common goals with all our energy. And it is only when these conditions are met that we are capable of managing people in a way that meets their needs and in the process elicits their performance, and that we experience close customer relationships.[38]

---

[37] Ultimately, the idea of a conscience is not speculative and, conceptually, not vaguer than concepts such as "happiness" or "satisfaction," let alone ones like "the greatest happiness of the greatest number" or "the greatest benefit to the greatest number." Furthermore, these concepts, hard to define in themselves, are still connected to the claim of rationality, which has long since proved not to lend itself to generalization.

[38] Heinrich Anker, *Balanced Valuecard: Leistung statt Egoismus* [Value balance in business: performance rather than self-interest] (Bern: Haupt Verlag, 2010), 72.

When we have achieved this, our conscience is not an obstacle but rather a prerequisite—it becomes our inner compass.

3.2.4 Self-Transcendence: Mankind and the Question of Meaning

By stepping outside ourselves, thus turning our gaze away from ourselves and looking beyond our own lives into the world, an ever-widening circle of the greater whole opens up for us. First we become aware of the other that is our mother and father; soon we encounter those people close to us—significant others. Then we meet groups of people— generalized others, our surrounding social world, mankind, the natural environment, the universe, and ultimately the transcendent world and, for many people, also God or the presence of a divinity, which in the human experience definitively transcends space and time.

The more we turn our focus away from ourselves and from our natural instincts and psychological drives, the further we step beyond ourselves. According to philosophical anthropology, this is self-transcendence, the second fundamental ability of the human spirit. The more we step beyond ourselves in terms of self-transcendence, the wider our horizon becomes, and the more the world opens up for us. The more pressing is the question of how we can remain faithful to our thoughts, feelings, and actions, and wherein our orientation, safety, and perhaps even certainty lie. In other words, we ask ourselves what the system is that coordinates us and where we find ourselves within this system.

Becoming aware of the world opening up to us is synonymous with our humanization, the awakening of mankind and humanity in general. This was the point in time when we suddenly started asking such questions as *Where do we come from? Who are we? Why and for what purpose are we here? Why must we die?* For parents, it is one of the most intense and poignant experiences when the world begins to open up for their children, when a child starts discovering the world him- or herself. It is during this time when our children keep us on our toes all the day long, at times driving us to the brink of madness with this one question: "Daddy, why …?" and "Mommy, what for …?" And in asking these questions, our children are not imitating somebody, as they are often inclined to do; this question stems from their innermost selves.

Questions as to why and what for are questions about meaning—*there is no single fundamental human need greater than the need to find meaning*. In mankind's wide world, "meaning" is the pivotal point for our understanding of ourselves and our world, the reference point of our thinking, feeling, and action. This also means that we humans are only completely at one with ourselves and fully capable of acting when we really experience the meaning of our deeds and our actions, when we can give them a meaningful place in our world—when we *understand* what we are doing.

In chapter 3.2.2, we looked at the first existential human need: that of *recognition by the you* by other people. Now we have identified the human desire for meaning as our second existential need. This brings us to a crucial point regarding the issue of performance and motivation:

> If you require people to perform, you have to offer them opportunities to experience meaning and recognition in return.

Here, "meaning" specifically refers to the meaning of our actions and ultimately our lives. "Recognition" refers to the meaning of our existence as an individual, which we experience in encountering other people. In a sense, this gives us confirmation that we exist as an independent individual. The meaning of our existence and the meaning of our actions are mutually reinforcing. Without experiencing a sense of existence, it is difficult to imbue our own actions with a sense of meaning. In turn, we gain a sense of the meaning of our own lives through our actions when we experience them as having an effect.

3.3 Societal Values: Our Most Important Source of Meaning

As a corporate culture audit, the focus of the Value Balance in Business is on employees' perception of meaning as well as their experience of recognition and appreciation—it addresses the most fundamental and thus also the most enduring aspects of human motivation. It is therefore pertinent that we now take a closer look at the concept of meaning. Viktor Frankl points us in an interesting direction by comparing the *search* for meaning[39] with a well-known process in psychology—that of "gestalt perception."[40] In gestalt perception, a figure is understood to stand out from its background. Something similar happens in the search for meaning, but in the gestalt sense of meaning, we do not merely perceive a "figure" that jumps out at us from a "background" but rather:

> What we perceive in the search for meaning is this: against the background of reality there is a possibility – the possibility of changing reality in some way or another.[41]

The meaning inherent in a situation becomes evident to us when we realize: "I personally can and must do something here!" Frankl's explanation of how we find meaning leads us to societal values. Societal values "tell" us what the reality *is* and at the same time what it *ought to be*—that is to say, the direction in which it must be changed.

Societal values convey to us which act or omission is desired of us in any given situation—in other words, which actions are expected of us and which actions we can expect and demand from others. Societal values make it possible for individuals to orient themselves in any situation and align their actions to a desirable social state or a desired outcome. This is achieved because they inform us of which action or behavior is "important," which is "unimportant," and which should be avoided in any given situation.

---

[39] Frankl speaks expressly of *finding* meaning and not of *giving* meaning, because he believes meaning to be something that is objective, something that is inherent in a situation and that must be discovered. By contrast, *giving* meaning would be the arbitrary act of ascribing a meaning, which could also be constructed in hindsight. See Viktor Frankl, *Der Wille zum Sinn* [The will to meaning: foundations and applications of logotherapy]. 4th edition (Munich: Piper, 1997), 25f.

[40] Frankl, *Der Wille zum Sinn*, 26f.

[41] Viktor Frankl, *Psychotherapie in der Praxis* [Psychotherapy in practice]. 3rd edition (Munich/Zurich: Piper, 1995), 29f.

3.3.1 Values: Generators of Tension and Catalysts for Action

One example of an important value in democratic countries is "equality before the law." When this principle is not fulfilled, laws are increasingly disregarded, and society gradually disintegrates. In practice, this might mean, for example: "It is important for judges to deliver impartial judgments." Values have a normative side; they contain an ideal quality (the target). In this particular case, the judge must obey this ideal by delivering impartial judgments. Should a judge deliver a partisan judgment, the reality—that is to say, the situation as it actually is—does not correspond to the ideal. The value of "equality before the law" is violated, and there is now a divide between the situation as it is and how it ought to be. This divergence between current and target can be the cause or the reason for a person or a group of people—for example, the victim of a partisan judicial decision or representatives of human rights groups—to change reality in order to create a new current that corresponds more closely to the target, such as requesting that the judgment delivered by a lower court be revised by a higher court.

From this, we can deduce that societal values contain a category that indicates the ideal situation or a normative dimension. From this perspective of the target or ideal, we assess situations by whether or not the (current) reality corresponds to the target/ideal (or norm). Societal values create a margin between current and target, and the greater this margin or divide between current and target, the more likely we are to be compelled to act in order to change the current to make it correspond more closely to the target. This action is the second and pragmatic dimension of societal values. It ultimately gives meaning to our actions—or more precisely, it allows us to experience our actions as being meaningful (fig. 5).

The more we are aligned with a societal value, the more we are motivated to reduce the tension between current and target states. The range of societal values that motivate us is nearly endless. In addition to equality before the law, there is, for example, respect for life itself, human dignity, health, mobility, freedom, accountability, personal responsibility, charity, education, peace, technological progress, loyalty, dependability, trustworthiness, valor, human respect, the sanctity of nature, tolerance, a receptiveness to the rest of the world, security, performance, wisdom, reciprocity, truth, honesty, and so on.[42]

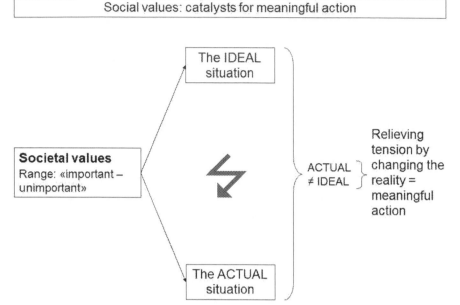

Figure 5. We use societal values as a basis to assess whether a situation is as it ought to be or not. The more the current situation diverges from target situation, the more likely it is that we will change reality in order to relieve the tension between current and target. Such action is experienced as being meaningful: meaning is found in action.

3.3.2 Values: A Guide for Good

The target or ideal aspect of values describes a desirable situation or an action that is evaluated as being positive. When we base our actions on values and thus commit ourselves to these, we feel that we are good for someone (if we are dealing with people) or that we are good for something (if we choose to stand up for groups of people or a larger whole, like the sanctity of nature, or an ideal or a societal value such as justice).

---

[42] In contrast to happiness or satisfaction, values are intersubjective categories and as such offer business a much more reliable basis as a network of exchange relationships than do such concepts as the pursuit of personal benefit or happiness or the pursuit of the greatest benefit or the greatest happiness for the greatest number of people.

The meaning that our work has and the motivation associated with this result in part from the experience of being *good for someone*—spouse, children, clients, colleagues, superiors—or *good for something*—an ideal such as health, technological progress, education, truth, and the like. At the same time, we are making a contribution to changing the reality, and with our actions, we embrace this; we feel that we actively shape it and that we are a part of it. This represents personal fulfillment and meaning in the highest and most human sense. It is built on the idea of service, of coevolution and cocreation: "To be good for someone" and "to be good for something" means to be willing to perform our tasks, here and now.

It is our awareness of values that reveals to us which changes to reality are needed, which tasks await us, what the current situation is that we strive to bring closer to the target and in this way can and should convert into a new current. This allows us to do justice to reality and to life, thereby becoming the architects of our own lives and in the process giving our work content and intrinsic value. This value goes far beyond that which the self-serving standard theory of economics and its notion of work abstracting largely from meaning and content (of work) ascribes to this concept—which is what has resulted in approximately 80 percent of all employees worldwide having merely a weak relationship with their work, if they have one at all. This is because in a self-serving economy, work is only understood as a means to enable consumption and payment as compensation for having endured the burden of working.

3.3.3 Values: Sources of Our Ability and Willingness to Perform

To place oneself at the service of values, to be good for someone or something, is synonymous with the concept of performance. This brings us back to the work of Peters and Waterman, Kotter and Heskett, Collins and Porras, and Joyce, Nohria and Roberson (see chapter 2). We saw that companies that achieved long-term success have two common denominators:

1. They treat their employees with respect.
2. They place a prime on performance (i.e., they are "good for someone or something" in terms of values and meaning).

This provides us with an initial indication of *why* these criteria are important to companies for achieving long-term success. They correspond to the two most fundamental, existential needs of mankind—they speak to the core of humanity and to meaning and recognition. Only when these needs are met are employees willing and able to give their best. If you require people to perform, you have to offer them meaning and recognition in return. Later, we will look in more detail at what this means for the company.

3.3.4 Values: A Closer Look

By aligning their lives with societal values, individuals place themselves at the service of a larger social whole. Yet individuals are anything but merely functions of their societies:

- By stepping outside themselves, people are able to emancipate themselves from their natural urges and, in terms of values and norms, from the expectations of other people or those of society. Because individuals have free will, they can decide whether they wish to act in accordance with what they consider to be meaningful and what not.[43]
- Individuals who can step outside themselves and transcend themselves are not subservient to societal directives. While it is true that meaningful action on the one hand presupposes society (and its values) as a guide, a free society legitimizes itself by serving the individual and its free will. Meaning is the link between individuals and society (and by the same virtue, also between individuals and companies).
- At the same time, there also exists a variety of values in open societies that are to a certain extent contradictory. It is up to the ethical, absolutely unique conscience of every individual to decide which values they ultimately allow themselves to be led by and what meaning they want to achieve through their actions.

---

[43] We have an impressive example in Nelson Mandela: in twenty-seven years of detention as a political prisoner, he never yielded. Physically, he was behind bars, but he did not allow his spirit to be taken from him. Thus Mandela held on to the last of his freedoms—the freedom of opinion.

By choosing the values we want to serve, we make use of our freedoms and our responsibilities and thus shape ourselves, our personality, our identity, and our world.

- We only experience societal values as meaningful and motivating if we can choose them freely; values that are imposed on us come with constraints and as such are not a source of meaning. They do not endure in the long run; people withdraw from them, engage in passive resistance, or actively oppose them.

- People and thus also employees do not simply allow others to prescribe meaning to them or otherwise dupe them into accepting that a company inevitably offers true opportunities for experiencing meaning.

- From this point of view, every individual has the freedom and responsibility to decide which offer of meaning they choose to accept as an employee—and from which company. For companies and other performance-based organizations, this means that, in the future, they will face increasingly intense competition in the search for employees. They will have to express their thoughts on the issue of meaning and value ever more clearly and confidently and not just profess to certain values but actually live them. In the future, projecting a glossy image that serves only as window dressing but is not truly lived will simply no longer suffice. This is consistent with the fact (see chapter 3.1) that 80 percent of all employees indicate a preference for ethical and socially responsible businesses.

The following three points regarding values should also be mentioned:

1. Even "businesses" like the Cosa Nostra are held together by values—there is honor among thieves too. However, their values fail to bear up to the questions, *Would I want to be on the receiving end of my actions?* and *Do I want my actions to become the general rule that applies to me too?* Only if we can answer yes to these questions may we presume to act meaningfully. As beings that are capable of feeling empathy, we are in a position to answer these questions.

2. We have come to understand our ethical conscience as our ultimate guiding force. However, if we regard this as an absolute, we run the risk of being led astray into dramatic or fanatical acts,

and thus we must continuously test our conscience by asking ourselves the questions in point 1.

3. Beauty, material wealth, prestige, power, and so on can also be societal values. Only those values that serve to make us look beyond ourselves and be good for someone or something are real, meaningful values. If they are merely an end in themselves, they are nothing more than pseudo-values, and then they are not fit to be a sustainable source of meaning and motivation.

3.4 Philosophical Anthropology, Meaning-Centered Psychology, and the Natural Sciences: A Meeting of the Minds

Philosophical anthropology and meaning-centered psychology must be placed on an entirely different level from that of neurobiology and evolution theory as natural sciences. However, it is extremely interesting to note that each of these disciplines arrives at conclusions that are based on free will, the capacity for freedom and responsibility, and a respect for the other and for cooperation rather than crude self-interest—as well as on the need for meaning and recognition and the role these play as a motivational force.

From a neurobiological perspective, Joachim Bauer[44] writes the following on meaning and recognition:

> If recognition, attentiveness and trust are the neurobiological fuel of motivation systems, where does this fuel come from? ... It comes from a single source: interpersonal relationships. ... Motivation as a basic attitude is also greatly affected by whether people feel that their work and that which they are working for are in essence meaningful. A commercial enterprise is "meaningful" when it ultimately serves goals that are useful to society – in other words, cooperative goals. ... Where the question of a higher purpose of economic activity is looked at from the executive level, potential

---

[44] Joachim Bauer, *Prinzip Menschlichkeit: Warum wir von Natur aus kooperieren* [A principle of humanity: why we are naturally cooperative]. 5th edition (Hamburg: Hoffmann und Campe, 2007), 190, 204f.

is especially activated if crises or temporary phases of hardship need to be bridged within a company. To see in a convincing and understandable way why a decision that is unpleasant in the short term had to be taken can be a key motivational impulse.

Gerald Hüther, a neurobiologist like Joachim Bauer, describes the development and performance potential that is associated with recognition of and cooperation between people:[45]

> Once you start thinking about which basic attitudes you would have to make your own in order to use your brain more comprehensively, with more complexity and more interconnectedness than ever before, a whole host of other concepts [in addition to mindfulness and caution] comes to mind ...: meaningfulness, sincerity, modesty, prudence, truthfulness, reliability, commitment ... The only thing you need is other people with whom you can share your perceptions, your feelings, your experiences and your knowledge.

Revelations from recent research in evolutionary biology are equally fascinating. Gerhard Neuweiler writes:[46]

> Evolution is a grand and captivating story of the emancipation of life from the tight constraints of nature toward an increasingly self-determined freedom, and the climax of this story of emancipation is mankind.

By analogy, Neuweiler describes mankind's position in the world as follows:

– Only mankind is able to create a world of its own based on freely chosen criteria.

---

[45] Gerald Hüther, *Bedienungsanleitung für ein menschliches Gehirn* [The compassionate brain: a revolutionary guide to developing your intelligence to its full potential]. 6th edition (Göttingen: Vandenhoeck & Ruprecht, 2006), 123f.
[46] Neuweiler, *Und wir sind es doch*, 200f.

- We are the only living beings able to escape the dictate of reproductive fitness and natural selection.
- Only mankind is able to mold natural evolution through a cultural evolution based on predetermined objectives (coevolution being the operative word).
- We alone have acquired self-determination with this freedom and thus bear responsibility for all life.
- We alone know, because we as individuals are self-conscious beings, that each person's life ends in death—and, faced with death, we create transcendent concepts of the world with which to define life.
- For Neuweiler, the human being is the "freest and most fascinating creature that ever inhabited the globe. In mankind, living matter has been set free."

It is very interesting that theories from philosophical anthropology and meaning-centered psychology align with insights from the field of natural sciences. It indicates that there is a cross-disciplinary paradigm shift from reductionist and deterministic concepts of humanity, such as that of the *Homo economicus*, toward one that leaves space for meaning, freedom, and responsibility. In other words, it takes into account the special status humans have by comparison to all other living things, and thus, in the sense of coevolution and cocreation, it gives freedom and coresponsibility to mankind once again. When viewed from this perspective, the standard theory of economics, with its paradigm of self-interest, cuts an old and lonely picture in the world of science.

3.5 The Human Spirit—A Unique, Irreplaceable, and Inexhaustible Resource

We have explored the motivation theory on which the Value Balance in Business is based in some depth by examining and differentiating it from the utilitarian standard theory of economics, with its soulless *Homo economicus*. This was done in part with the intention of laying bare the Value Balance in Business's performance- and motivation-based principles and opening it up to criticism. It was also carried out to reveal which performance potential is capable of being mobilized and used as a comparative advantage by companies that are driven by long-term performance objectives—potential which primarily self-interested companies do not utilize and which they also do not accredit to their employees as performance.

> The Value Balance in Business aims to make a significant contribution to the development of the kind of human potential that is the source of long-term, above-average profitability for companies; enhanced value for the company starts with an increase in appreciation for its employees. It concerns mankind's unique gift of spirit and the related human ability which, if the future is to belong to coevolution, cannot be allowed to lie fallow—neither for the sake of the people nor for the sake of the performance of companies and the economy. In other words, it concerns entrepreneurship that places itself at the service of customers and society. It is characterized by a willingness to perform, communications-oriented management relations, a willingness to cooperate in favor of common overarching objectives, customer focus, creativity, a tendency toward innovation and change, task rather than power orientation, mutual commitment and trust, loyalty to the company's mission, vision, and values, and the willingness to share responsibility for the prosperity of the company.

In accordance with meaning-centered psychology and philosophical anthropology, the three dimensions of mankind (mind, body and spirit—see fig. 6) are continuously interacting with each other, and it is in the tangible form of this interaction that each person's individuality and uniqueness lie. Conversely, this means that humanity is only possible if the third, spiritual dimension can come into play. When this is made possible for employees, they reward their employers with a marked willingness to perform and with cooperation and understanding, both within the company and with its customers, as well as responsible use of the freedoms and responsibilities they are granted. In doing so, their performance is characterized by values, empathy, and conscience. And only where it is possible for us to look beyond ourselves, where we do not merely respond to our instincts and psychological urges like *Homo economicus* and are not bound to these,[47] can real creativity exist. This is the ability to think

---

[47] Through structures and processes, management tools, motivation initiatives, and the like.

beyond the current situation by stepping outside the self and transcending the self to see things anew and combine them in new ways, in cooperation with and at the service of the customer. "Go the other way!"

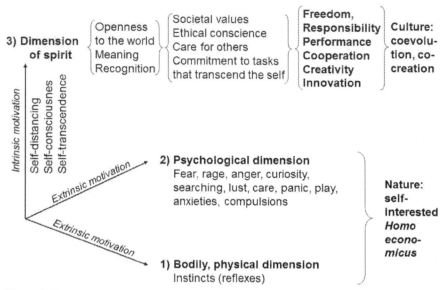

Figure 6. The Value Balance in Business is based on a three-dimensional image of mankind, thereby offering a motivation concept that goes well beyond regarding employees as resources, which is based on the idea of the self-interested Homo economicus and related motivation concepts.

Societal values are an important catalyst for creating a spirit of innovation: with their dual aspect of current and target, they are causal in human action. When managers attach innovation and change processes to values and the divergence between current and target, employees gain insight into their own meaning and become willing to bridge this current-target gap through their own actions. In this case, the chances of successfully implementing innovation and change projects are much greater than when merely attempting to affect these projects through changes at the level of employees' action and behavior (see fig. 1).

This book is not about playing off mankind's spiritual dimension against the physical and psychological dimensions but rather about helping to restore the spiritual dimension to the importance it deserves—in economics, in theory, in teaching and consulting, and in everyday business—and not just because it is primarily what makes human beings human but rather because it concerns a fundamentally important question regarding the ability of companies and the economy to perform, including to the benefit of society.

However, the following points must be noted in particular:

1. Meaning and recognition are not just needs like any other needs; they are existential in that they relate to humanity itself. Seen in this light, the need for meaning is not at the top of the famous pyramid of needs that Abraham Maslow postulated; it is not a need that only comes into play once people's natural and social needs are satisfied. On the contrary, it comes first; it is what constitutes humanity. Maslow himself clearly also saw it as such: "I agree entirely with Frankl, that man's primary concern is his will to meaning."[48]

2. Because of its existential significance, there is nothing that can replace meaning. According to Elisabeth Lukas

    > ... for the sake of having a meaningful role, people are prepared ... to make sacrifices and, if necessary, to leave some needs unsatisfied. Physical and mental well-being play a secondary role in the search for meaning. By contrast, a failure in the search for meaning cannot be offset by any kind of physical and psychological well-being whatsoever ...[49]

3. Should the answers to *why?* and *for whom?* fail to materialize— those things that make us look beyond ourselves and give us meaning and motivation—then our lives will revolve around ourselves like that of the *Homo economicus* of standard

---

[48] Comments on Dr. Frankl's paper, "Reading in Humanistic Psychology," published by A. J. Sutich and M. A. Vich (New York: 1969), quoted as per Frankl, *Der Wille zum Sinn*, 181.

[49] Elisabeth Lukas, *Lehrbuch der Logotherapie* [Logotherapy textbook: meaning-centered psychotherapy]. (Munich/Vienna: Profil 1998), 39.

economics, around our own physical and mental dimensions, our own sensibilities—and then we are in danger of being thrown back on ourselves and becoming addicted to ourselves. The spiritual dimension as the only dimension that is really human can then no longer come into play. Possible consequences of such a void, a vacuum of meaning (in which our capacity for distancing and transcending ourselves is blocked) include envy, aggression, addictions to drugs, gambling, risk and consumerism, a craving for recognition, and a greed for power and money. Companies that live a culture of performance primacy and respect for the dignity of their employees can spare themselves a great deal of conflict and power struggle, which would otherwise rob employees of joy and harm the company.[50] The Value Balance in Business is thus not merely meant to mobilize untapped resources but also to remove barriers within companies that hinder or even block their efforts.

4. Meaning is not just a fair-weather friend—it carries employees and companies through crises—especially so. Nietzsche put it in a nutshell: "He who has a Why to live for can bear almost any How."

"when this goes hand in hand with appreciation for people in companies," as we would like to add. Under these conditions, in times of crisis, employees are willing to accommodate their company and to commit to its well-being in many ways instead of abandoning it as soon as possible.

---

[50] These could have dramatic repercussions: one US study claims that destructive, unsocial behavior can lead to a significant breakdown in the performance of those on the receiving end of such behavior from their colleagues. According to a survey among thousands of executives and employees in the United States, 48 percent of those affected reduced their commitment to their work, 47 percent reduced their working hours, 38 percent spoke of a decline in the quality of their work, 66 percent said their performance had declined, 80 percent lost time during processing of corresponding incidents, 63 percent lost time in an effort to avoid the aggressor, and 78 percent said their loyalty to the company have suffered. See Christine Porath and Christine Pearson, "How Toxic Colleagues Corrode Performance," *Harvard Business Review* (April 2009).

3.6 Three Main Avenues toward Meaning

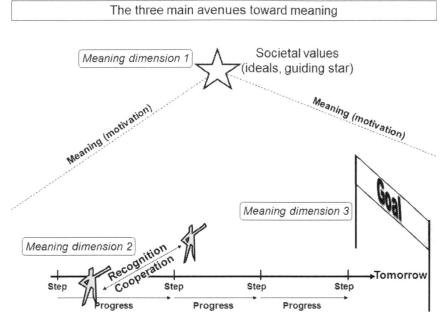

The three main avenues toward meaning

Figure 7. *Societal values, recognition by the other, and ambitious goals—our three main sources of meaning that can complement and reinforce each other.*

Dimensions of meaning 2 and 3 substantiate the first dimension of meaning.

There are three main avenues for finding meaning identified in the Value Balance in Business:

1. *Societal values:* These allow us to look beyond ourselves and integrate our actions into a social context or a social space. They give us answers to the questions we ask ourselves in our search for meaning: *Who/what am I good for? Who/what are my actions good for?*
2. The second source of existential meaning that we have presented and actively expressed is *recognition* from other people—positive interaction with the other.
3. A third relevant source of meaning is *ambitious, long-term goals* that require our attention and our energy. They are the end point

of a time axis along which we can meaningfully integrate each step and every action we take toward this goal. Our goals give every single step a "why" that carries meaning. If these goals also involve societal values or a relationship with other people, their motivating effect is compounded.

On dimension of meaning 1: Societal values are not restricted to time or space. As ideals, they ultimately remain an unrealizable standard. This is exactly why they serve as reliable, long-term guiding stars— fixed points by which we can orient our actions and behavior. To some extent, they are the reference points for our human capacity for self-transcendence. To a great degree, they allow us to look beyond ourselves and orient ourselves with something outside us. They even outshine dimensions of meaning 2 and 3, although it is in their association with these dimensions that they gain substance.

As we have seen, societal values structure our actions and behavior, creating predictability and certainty around our actions. As shared ideals, they also create a sense of unity and belonging.

Within communities of individuals that share the same societal values, they remove barriers and bring them closer together. The downside of this situation is that the values that are shared within an organization, a community, or a society can build boundaries between them and the outside world. As we saw in chapter 3.2.3, our receptiveness to the world makes it possible for our understanding of each other to transcend borders, not just in a vague sense of tolerance but in the realization that we as human beings constitute a unity within our diversity. Our differences do not represent a threat but rather an opportunity and our fortune. They are one of the secrets of evolution, of creativity, of the search for something even better and even more functional; they are drivers of development and growth throughout the economy and in each individual company.

On dimension of meaning 2: What makes us feel that we are being taken seriously and appreciated as a person? Joachim Bauer formulates the following prerequisites for successful human relationships:[51]

---

[51] Bauer, *Prinzip Menschlichkeit*, 190ff.

1. *See and be seen:* We want to be recognized and treated as individuals.
2. *Mutual attention:* We have a need for our interaction partners to show an interest in our concerns and in that which is important to us.
3. *Emotional resonance:* The willingness to absorb our interaction partners' moods, putting ourselves in their situations, and acting appropriately brings us another step closer to each other; mutual involvement creates common ground.
4. *Shared action:* Doing something tangible with other people, tackling it ourselves and not just delegating it is, according to Bauer, often totally underestimated—and yet it is an approach that plays a big role in building relationships.
5. *Understanding the motives and intentions* of our interaction partners: This is the most important element in relationships. From the perspective of meaning-centered psychology, it is here that the human capacity for distancing and transcending ourselves is most pronounced. This is what makes understanding and mutual agreement possible.

The more effectively interpersonal relationships function, the more we also agree on the values that guide us and on our ambitious goals, and the more fruitful is our collaboration. Dimensions of meaning 1 and 3 lend content and purpose to dimension of meaning 2.

On dimension of meaning 3: Ambitious, challenging goals contain a target—a future desirable situation—that challenges our creative minds and leads us to peak performance, thereby allowing us to grow beyond ourselves. The clearer, more attractive, and more tangible an image of the future state we have, the more likely this is to take place. Such an ambitious goal creates a time line along which individual steps toward this goal can be integrated meaningfully.

Such goals become even more attractive if they serve to substantiate dimensions of meaning 1 and 2.

3.7 Is It Meaning We Seek ... or Happiness?

Standard economic theory states that through the pursuit of our greatest personal happiness—or in business, in the search for own maximum benefit—we make the greatest contribution to the greatest happiness or benefit of the greatest number. This idea is at the heart of the utilitarian utopia. But it is interesting to note that John Stuart Mill, one of its protagonists, later questioned the foundations upon which the theory is built. In his autobiography, published in 1873 (the year he died), he wrote: "Ask yourself whether you are happy, and you cease to be so."[52]

Happiness seems to evade those who pursue it; in the long term, we cannot selectively induce, buy, or manipulate feelings of happiness. John Stuart Mill suffered a severe psychological crisis before he eventually arrived at this realization. Viktor Frankl provides an explanation for this—happiness is not self-contained; happiness cannot deliberately bring itself into existence.

> The more a person concerns himself with pleasure, the more it recedes. The more he pursues happiness, the more it eludes him. To understand this, we have to overcome the popular misconception that happiness is one of man's basic wants. What he actually wants is a cause that allows him to be happy. Once a cause has been established, the feeling of happiness will appear of its own accord. To the extent, however, that man aims at happiness directly, he loses sight of established cause, and the feeling of happiness will collapse in itself. In other words, happiness is a by-product and cannot be approached directly ...[53]

Mankind's primary drive is not for happiness or contentment. This assumption, the current utilitarian standard theory of economics, is as untenable as postulating that human beings have a natural social

---

[52] John Stuart Mill, *Autobiography* (London/New York/Toronto: Oxford University Press, 1952), 120f.
[53] Viktor Frankl, *Der Mensch vor der Frage nach dem Sinn* [Mankind and the question of meaning]. 10th edition. (Munich/Zurich: Piper, 1995), 228.

instinct that transforms the pursuit of our own happiness into the greatest happiness for the greatest number of people.

According to meaning-centered psychology, what is true for human happiness and contentment also applies to success. Viktor Frankl explains:

> Don't aim at success—the more you aim at it and make it a target, the more you are going to miss it. For success, like happiness, cannot be pursued; it must ensue, and it only does so as the unintended side effect of one's personal dedication to a cause greater than oneself or as the by-product of one's surrender to a person other than oneself. Happiness must happen, and the same holds for success: you have to let it happen by not caring about it. I want you to listen to what your conscience commands you to do and go on to carry it out to the best of your knowledge. Then you will live to see that in the long run—in the long run, I say!—success will follow you precisely because you had forgotten to think of it.[54]

What we have found with respect to businesses and their success (see fig. 2) obviously also applies for us as individuals: in the long run, happiness and success come about as the results of our performance through our commitment to tasks greater than ourselves. In other words, ultimately happiness and success reside in a focus on societal values or in concentrating on the *you*, on other people—happiness and success are the result of meaningful action and our search for meaning (fig. 8).

Among employees, the motivation theory outlined here mobilizes such forces as willpower, the willingness to cooperate, the ability to deal responsibly with freedom, creativity, innovation, and a willingness to change and adapt. Under the standard theory of economics with its pursuit of self-interest,

---

[54] Viktor Frankl, *Man's Search for Meaning* (New York: Washington Square Press, 1985), 16f.

these attributes all remain unused, because this approach obscures the individual's spiritual dimension completely (fig. 6). Since *Homo economicus* does not have these abilities, they are simply overlooked. When employees are managed according to the maxim lived by *Homo economicus*—in other words, as a primarily self-serving and not as a primarily meaning-oriented being—these forces wither progressively. It is thus not only at the level of the company (see chapter 2.3) but also at the level of the individual that the paradigm of maximization of self-interest greatly affects the performance potential inherent in people and businesses. This paradigm is therefore not a good basis for the successful creation of shared value. Shared value thrives best within the context of a motivation theory that offers room enough for the primal human need for meaning and recognition.

Task – meaning – motivation – performance: the path to happiness and success or: Happiness must ensue, you cannot pursue it …

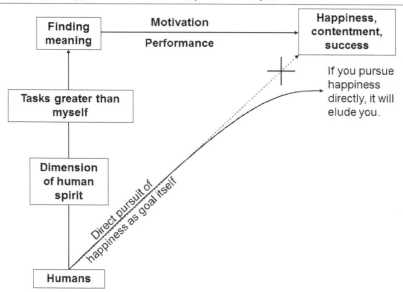

Figure 8. There is just as little chance of a shortcut to success (and to happiness) for people as there is for businesses. Success happens as a result of services that are rendered, not as a result of controlling or even manipulating success in itself.

It is not success that primarily brings about happiness and contentment—it actually works the other way around.

> When we feel that our actions have meaning, when we recognize that we ourselves and the things that we do mean something for someone or something, and when in the process we experience recognition from others, it is then that we are mentally and psychologically willing and able to do our best. This—the knowledge and the experience of "a job well done"—is a source of happiness and contentment,[55] and our willingness to do our best forms a sound basis for our success.

As noted in the introduction, it is for this reason that the Value Balance in Business, in its culture and motivation model as well as in audits based on this model, does not make the target variable the employees' contentment. Instead, it is their willingness to perform (depending on the degree of meaning experienced and the perceived appreciation). *This* is the source of success and happiness or contentment.

> As creatures with a desire for meaning, the narrow-minded, target-driven world of *Homo economicus* and the maximization of self-interest are too restricting for human beings—our real home is the world of societal (i.e., cultural) values; it is our source of meaning and the foundation upon which we build interpersonal relationships based on mutual recognition and reciprocity. When these conditions are met, we are mentally and psychologically willing and able to look beyond ourselves and our own interests and to give our best in the service of tasks that are greater than we are or that focus on our fellow humans.

This capacity is a fundamental characteristic of humanity. However, it is not just rooted in our natural impulses and instincts, as utilitarianism once assumed, but in the phenomenon of mankind's spiritual dimension and cultural world. If a company wants to make its employees feel truly at home

---

[55] See also Tatjana Schnell, "The Sources of Meaning and Meaning in Life Questionnaire (SoME): Relations to Demographics and Well-Being," *Journal of Positive Psychology* 4, no. 6 (2009): 483–499; and Sheryl Zika and Kerry Chamberlain, "On the Relation between Meaning in Life and Psychological Well-Being," *British Journal of Psychology* (1992), 133–145, quoted as per www.sinnforschung.org/aktuelle-beitrage 9721854218.

Heinrich Anker

and allow them to fully develop their strength and skills, it needs to engage with this world in the same way that the Value Balance in Business embraces it. This is one of the main reasons why performance and employee-oriented companies are, in the long term, economically superior to those that are focused on short-term maximization of profit. In this context, the creation of shared value represents more than just damage control; it actually provides a real service in the interest of both businesses and society.

3.8 *Homo Economicus* and Ethics

Homo economicus lives alone in a world driven by targets—where everything is subject to the maximization of self-interest. However, as meaning-centered beings, we do not live here but rather in the universe of societal values in which our aims are (usually) embedded. Where this is not the case, we find ourselves living in a world that is an end in itself—ultimately a world of nihilism. It is a world of emptiness, and there is a real risk that in this world the purpose justifies the means; striving for success for its own sake without embedding this effort in the context of societal values is pointless and destructive to business and industry, to individuals, to society, and to our natural environment.

Homo economicus attempts to justify its single-minded focus on purpose by referring to its contribution to the greatest benefit for the largest number of people. Apart from the fact that this concept does not work (as we have already shown), *Homo economicus* is certainly no democrat: it never asks economic and social subjects wherein they see the greatest benefit themselves. It simply straps people into the straitjacket of price and quantity and binds them to supposedly scientific (and thus unchangeable) laws, such as "The market demands it" and "The competition is forcing us." These stereotypes, which come from the arsenal of the self-interested standard theory of economics, hide the fact that markets are made by people and can thus also be shaped by people—and that we are ultimately responsible for the market and its results. Peter Drucker: "Markets are not created by God, nature or economic force but by business people."[56]

---

[56] Drucker, *The Essential Drucker*, 15.

4. Meaning and the Company

The basic philosophy, spirit, and drive
of an organization have far more to
do with its relative achievements
than do technological or economic
resources, organizational structure,
innovation, and timing.
> —Thomas Watson Jr. (IBM)

4.1   How Meaning and Recognition Can Be Instilled into the Core of a Company

In chapter 2, we established through Peter Drucker[17] that if a company aims to exist over a long period of time and seeks to be highly profitable in the long term, it must place itself at the service of customers and society and, in this way, serve a meaningful purpose. Instead of making short-term profit maximization more important than anything else, companies that prosper in the long term must be good for someone or something from the point of view of customers and society.

In chapter 3, we saw that meaning and recognition, the experience of being good for someone or something, is of fundamental importance for the performance and commitment of employees and therefore also for the performance of the company. Nothing motivates people more than a desire for the kind of meaning that feeds the soul. Our next question is therefore, if companies must be good for someone or something from the perspective of customers and society on the one hand and from the point of view of employees on the other, how is this to be achieved?

A meaning- and performance-centered corporate philosophy and culture connect the employees' individual desire for meaning and the demands customers and society place on the company to fulfill a meaningful purpose in being good for someone or something.

61

We have already identified the three main avenues for finding meaning for people/employees as individuals (chapter 3.6):

1. Societal values (guiding star, ideal)
2. Long-term ambitious goals
3. Recognition by other people/interaction with the other

The three main avenues of companies to meaning and performance that benefit customers and society are thus closely related in terms of structure and content (see table 1). The core of a meaning- and performance-centered corporate philosophy and culture is formed by:

1. A mission (in the sense of an ideal—a high societal value)
2. A vision (long-term ambitious goals)
3. Societal values

The observation that these form the essential core for sustained successful entrepreneurship is confirmed by Collins/Hansen in their latest, empirically very broadly based study:

> Both Kelleher and Lewis, like all the 10Xers we studied, were nonconformists in the best sense. They started with value, purpose, long-term goals und severe performance standards; and they had the fanatic discipline to adhere to them.[57]

Here the term "purpose" corresponds to what we call "mission," and "long-term goals" correspond to the term "vision" as it is used here.

Mission, vision, and values are the core components of the Value Balance in Business as applied to a meaning- and performance-centered corporate culture. We can consider them the essence of a company's philosophy. They can be understood as central nuclei around which a company's culture is formed, just like the layers of a pearl are formed

---

[57] Jim Collins and Morten T. Hansen, *Great by Choice. Uncertainty, Chaos and Luck— Why Some Thrive Despite Them All* (New York: Harper Business, 2011), 23. The term "10Xers" refers to companies whose cumulative stock returns have exceeded those of their industry tenfold between 1972 and 2002.

around a grain of sand. Before we deal with them in more depth, here is a brief explanation of these concepts:

4.1.1   Mission, Ideal (Peter Drucker)

In focusing on a mission, the company looks beyond itself in the manner described by Peter Drucker.[17] A company's mission is its guiding star; it is the ideal that it follows and from which it derives and justifies its actions, both externally and internally. Its mission provides its societal values. The mission offers answers to such questions as *What is our reason for being? Why is it essential that we exist? How shall we place our company in the service of customers and society?* and *For what and/or whom will we be good?* The mission is not about a list of products and services; it is about the functions that the company fulfills for its customers and for society.

With reference to Peter Drucker, Malik demonstrates just how important a mission, in the form of an ideal, is for the functioning of an organization. A society functions if the individual can find status, function, a role, and tasks for him- or herself within it. Its power must be legitimized through participation by individuals and its anchoring in a higher ideal, in socially accepted values that are above laws and government actions.[58] Similarly, the company needs to be anchored in a higher ideal and the participation of its people in order to function properly.

4.1.2   Societal Values

a. External values:

Utility values: The appropriate values determine which direct benefits the company offers its customers and how it can and wants to best solve its customers' problems. The answer comes from asking the question,

---

[58] Fredmund Malik, "Konservativismus und effektives Management: Wege aus der Orientierungskrise" [Conservatism and effective management: ways out of the crisis of orientation] in *Kardinaltugenden effektiver Führung* [Cardinal virtues of effective management], eds. Peter Drucker and Peter Paschek (Frankfurt: Redline Wirtschaft, 2004), 33.

what problems does the customer want to solve with our help, or what meaning do our customers want to fulfill with our products? When taking this attitude, the company will consistently be sided with the customer in a way that transcends itself.

Relationship values with regard to customers: The appropriate values determine how the relationship with the customer should be shaped. When these relationships are lived, customers rate products to be of higher benefit.

Relationship values with regard to other stakeholders: The relationship with other stakeholders is also governed by certain values, as are dealings with shareholders, suppliers, authorities, institutions, and the media.

b. Internal values:

These values serve to ensure mutual recognition and appreciation among all employees. The question that identifies these values is, what is important to the employees, and what will make them feel appreciated and valued?

The criteria concerning appreciation in human interaction, formulated in chapter 3.6 with reference to Bauer, are also of fundamental importance here. However, companies can go much further here—for instance, in terms of allowing creative freedom at work, opportunities for participation, profit sharing, or programs for employee participation in the company. These all have a positive effect on the company's performance.

> There have now been a number of large and well-controlled studies—including those using before-and-after performance data for several hundred matched pairs of companies—which demonstrate the economic benefits of the combination of employee share-ownership and participation. These studies show repeatedly that substantial performance benefits come only when employee share-ownership schemes are accompanied by more participatory management methods. Research that

looked at a large number of British companies during the 1990s found that employee share-ownership, profit-sharing and participation each makes an independent contribution to increased productivity.[59]

4.1.3 Vision

A company's vision is a specific, long-term, challenging development goal that provides a purpose for people to give their best effort in collaboration with others. Just as with the company's mission and its values, it connects employees because it offers them a shared focus.

Vision and values provide more detail to the company's mission.

Avenues toward meaning for individuals (chapter 3)	Avenues toward meaning for companies (chapter 4)
The individual looks beyond the self (self-transcendence) and bases his or her actions on societal values, which serve as his or her guiding star or **ideal**.	**Mission or ideal** (in accordance with Peter Drucker): the company looks beyond itself and provides a service to customers and society. The ideal is a societal value.
Ambitious **goal** that allows an individual to grow beyond him- or herself.	**Vision** as a specific, ambitious, long-term development goal for a company to grow beyond itself.
A real **relationship with the Other**, with those around us, recognition, cooperation.	1. Internal **values**: These guide the interactions between all employees in terms of recognition, appreciation, and understanding 2. External **values**: These guide the interactions

---

[59] Wilkinson and Pickett, *The Spirit Level*, 256.

	3. a) With customers in two ways:
	– utility values (values from solutions that the company provides for customers' problems)
	– relationship values (shaping the relationship between customers and companies)
	b) With other stakeholders (suppliers, etc.)

Table 1. Analogies between the dimensions of meaning for individuals and companies.[60]

4.2 The Mission—Guiding Star of the Self-Transcendent Company

Many companies have a mission that gets them looking beyond themselves, take this mission seriously, and actively pursue it. These companies are extremely varied, from completely unknown to very well-known and respected organizations of all sizes and ownership structures. Here are some examples that cover a very broad spectrum:[61]

Nucor Corporation	There's work to be done in America. … Rebuilding and expanding our infrastructure … is the bridge back to being a nation that innovates, makes and builds things.
Hewlett-Packard:	To make technical contributions for the advancement and welfare of humanity
Walt Disney:	To make people happy
Sony:	To elevate the Japanese culture and national status
A school bus company:	Carrying our nation's future[62]

---

[60] Heinrich Anker, "Co-Evolution: Wealthier Together" in *Tendances Économiques et Sociales de la Valeur en Entreprise*, Valérie LeJeune (Paris : L'Harmattan, 2014), 150.

[61] Examples 2–4 quoted as per Collins and Porras, *Built to Last*; example 5 quoted as per Jim Clemmer, *The Leader's Digest: Timeless Principles for Team and Organization Success* (n.p.: TCG Press, 2003), 12.

[62] Clemmer, *The Leader's Digest*, 12.

Clemmer Group: We are here to make the world a better
                        place. Our overarching purpose is to make a
                        difference in each other's lives and in the lives
                        of those we serve.
A Swiss IT company: Unlimited communication

It is clear to see that these companies look beyond themselves in the
orientation of their mission and place themselves at the service of a
greater social whole in line with their social values. This brings us back to
Peter Drucker's quote in chapter 2.3: "Business enterprises—and public
service institutions as well—are organs of society. They do not exist for
their own sake, but to fulfill a specific social purpose and to satisfy a
specific need of a society, a community, or individuals. They are not ends
in themselves, but means."[17]

A particularly illustrative example of this is the well-known Swiss
company Ricola: "At Ricola, business success is not an end in itself.
Instead, the company uses its success as an incentive to act responsibly
toward all employees, society and the environment ... As a company in
touch with nature, Ricola sets great store by the excellent quality of the
ingredients used in its products. For example, it only uses herbs grown
under controlled, environmentally friendly conditions. These herbs are
not only more aromatic but also possess an inner strength—the healing
power of nature."[63]

In this example, the performance of a prosperous company to the benefit
of the environment—and therefore also society—is explicitly expressed.
This example also clearly shows that there is no contradiction between
making a contribution to the greater social whole and the need to make
a profit, but that these can instead stand in synergistic relation to each
other. With its naturally produced and therefore particularly flavorful
ingredients, the value that the company offers its customers in the
form of a delicious candy is based on societal value creation: on its
cultivation of ingredients using environmentally friendly methods. This
is coevolution in action.

---

[63] http://www.ricola.ch/index.cfm?12FEB724CF0246FEC967731DD96F597D9, March
16, 2010.

Heinrich Anker

The German company dm-Drogeriemarkt has a similar approach: compared to conventional products on the market, such store brands as Alana and Alverde natural cosmetics offer customers added value through their response to sustainability issues, and sustainability is a factor in the brand identity (quality and sustainability are what set the brand apart from its competitors).[64]

> This brings us to one of the core ideas of the shared-value approach as postulated by Porter/Kramer (see chapter 2.1.). This idea is very easily embedded in the concept of a meaning- and performance-centered corporate culture. In order to understand the full extent of the importance of shared value, the company needs to look beyond itself and focus on a mission, as it is put into practice in a meaning- and performance-centered corporate culture. Companies that place short-term maximization of profit above all else are by and large blind to the importance of shared value. They live in a world where the economic goal is an end in itself, while the world of societal values remains closed to them. The sooner a company starts to live a meaning- and performance-centered corporate culture, the better it is able to harness the full potential of shared value for the benefit of society as much as itself, as the example of Ricola illustrates. In this cultural context, the concept of shared value may still unfold and expand further, particularly in terms of sustainability.[65]

---

[64] Margrit Meyer and Jan Wassmann, "Strategische Corporate Social Responsibility: Konzeptionelle Entwicklung und Implementierung in der Praxis am Beispiel ,dm-drogerie markt'" [Strategic Corporate Social Responsibility: Conceptual Development and Implementation in Practice with the Example of 'dm-drogerie markt'], research papers on marketing strategy, no. 3/2011, http://hdl.handle.net/10419/44939.

[65] "Shared Value is not social responsibility, philanthropy, or even sustainability, but a new way to achieve economic success. It is not on the margin of what companies do but at the center"—Porter and Kramer, "Creating Shared Value." Porter/Kramer are right to argue that similar to a mission, shared value should not be based on traditional CSR ideas (often a form of modern indulgences for past corporate sins) or philanthropy, but above all on an awareness of the social integration of business and its associated responsibilities (as well as the associated economic opportunities)—the perception of social responsibility in itself is a huge step away from the paradigm of maximization of self-interest as it has been understood and practiced up to now. However, with their negative attitude toward sustainability, Porter/Kramer nevertheless fall short; this must

In summary, we have thus far determined the following: a mission is like a guiding star; wherever we are, we can orient ourselves by it—it is always there. Once we have chosen a specific guiding star, it remains fixed in its position; it cannot be manipulated by us. This makes our guiding star reliable, even if we brave stormy seas. Its effect is most strongly felt if everybody on the boat can see it and is guided by it. When this is the case, there is also a great deal of confidence that the goal can be achieved by joining forces; therefore, it makes sense to give the company our best, especially in times of crisis and periods of great change. As long as there is a reliable guiding star, as long as employees can expect that the spirit of the company as embodied by the ideal remains intact, almost everything else in the company can change. Under these conditions, employees are open to new ideas; they do not cling tightly to the current situation, current processes, structures, products, and their current status as if their lives depended on it. In turn, this is a good foundation for successfully implementing the concept of shared value in a company.

4.3 Vision: Tangible Objectives Are a Motivational Force That Leads to Tangible Results

Visions are images of an anticipated future—and the clearer and more memorable they are, the more relevant they will be in practice. According to Roberto Assagioli, this is because visions are a powerful force. "Images have great power and one could say that they constitute a necessary link between the will and other psychological functions"[66]

This is true both for individuals and for groups of people, such as a company's employees. Corporate visions have a long time horizon; they require thinking beyond current capabilities and power and the current environment of the organization. They transcend a company's tactical horizon and often its strategic horizon, as well. Although the opportunities to implement them should exist, they are not necessarily a safe bet. The loftier the visions, the more valuable and desirable they

---

be incorporated in the shared-value approach, or it stands to lose much of its future potential and the resulting attractiveness.

[66] Roberto Assagioli, *Die Schulung des Willens* [The training of the will] (Paderborn: 2003), 169.

appear; this in turn encourages motivation and creativity on the part of the employees, especially if these visions fall within the context of the mission. As with a mission, a vision brings together the employees of a company and strengthens their desire to cooperate.

Below are some examples to illustrate how visions can get to the heart of the matter in an attractive and effective way:

- "We are the BBC of Switzerland!" (Schweizer Radio DRS—a Swiss radio station)
- "We want to become the Harvard of the West!" (Stanford University, California, 1940)[67]
- "We want to become the dominant player in commercial aircraft and bring the world into the jet age." (Boeing, 1950)[67]

4.4   Values: What Is Important Is Valuable; What Is Valuable Is Meaningful

The Value Balance in Business makes a distinction between internal and external values. Internal values primarily serve to ensure mutual respect and recognition within the company. They reinforce the commonalities or sense of identity that result from living a shared mission and pursuing a common vision, and they create trust as well as certainty around expectations and actions. External values determine the benefits (utility) the company offers its customers with its product(s) and how it aims to shape its relations with customers and other stakeholders.

Examples of internal values:

Swiss Radio DRS: Mutual respect and goodwill
                             We communicate openly, directly,
                             and honestly
                             Individual responsibility and initiative

---

[67] Quoted as per Collins and Porras, *Built to Last*.

The Swiss branch of a major enterprise:	Mutual respect, teamwork, individual initiative
A Swiss educational institute:	Open-mindedness, tolerance, mutual respect, humor, mutual growth

Examples of (external) utility and relationship values:

Swiss Radio DRS:	Respect for people's dignity, credibility, reliability, and fairness (relationship values); current, independent, unbiased (utility values)
The Swiss branch of a major enterprise:	The customer is king, reliability (relationship values), innovation (utility value)
TRISA:	"We at TRISA are grateful that we can produce useful and sensible products (relationship value) that provide pleasure and well-being (utility values)."
Victorinox:	"Our effort to provide our fellow human beings all over the world with practical, functional, reasonably priced and top-quality products (utility values) gives our lives deeper meaning (relationship value) and makes our work even more pleasurable and satisfying."

Heinrich Anker

4.5 On the Function and Effect of a Company's Mission, Vision, and Values

A company's mission, vision, and values permanently broaden, deepen, and reinforce the horizon and perception of meaning as experienced by its employees—it acts as an agency for meaning. If a company places itself at the service of its customers and society through its mission, vision, and values, it offers employees the meaningful experience of being good for someone or something through their work in the company. Through its mission, vision, and values, a company incorporates the meaning that it provides to customers and society into its character. In this way, it widens the horizons of meaning and motivation for its employees— attributes that remain entirely lacking in a company whose goal is maximizing short-term profit. Meaning is motivation; when a company lives with performance as its primary motive, motivational forces that remain unused in self-serving companies are unleashed (fig. 9).

> A meaning- and performance-centered corporate culture enriches the meaningful aspect of employees' tasks and intensifies the sense of their own reason for being, the feeling and the knowledge of being able to contribute something positive and the idea of being good for someone or something. In other words, a company's mission, vision, and values give new qualities to the *why* and *for whom* questions in employees' work— they experience a substantial broadening and reinforcement in their perspective on meaning and the associated commitment they feel.

It may well be possible for a company that is preoccupied with itself and with primarily maximizing its own profit to find meaning if we consider our material compensation (which most of us need to a certain extent), and if we consider team focus and the like. However, when it comes to meaningful self-transcendence by a company (the mission), a focus on motivational and ambitious goals (the vision), and recognition of people (the values), the self-interested company simply cannot keep up in terms of motivation and commitment, and the most human of human resources are squandered at the expense of people, the company, the industry, and society.

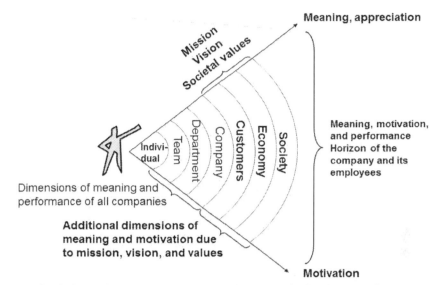

| Mission, vision, and values boost meaning and motivation |

Figure 9. Mission, vision, and values boost meaning and motivation. Because of a company's mission, vision, and values, the customers, the economy, and—above all—society are all within the focus of the employees. The employees' view extends beyond the company; it opens up additional opportunities for them to be good for someone or something; and their scope of meaning and their motivation expands accordingly.

From the employees' perspective, a meaning- and performance-centered corporate culture such as the one on which the Value Balance in Business is based allows the company to act as a lever that significantly enhances their effectiveness and their contribution to shaping reality—regardless of whether it is a small company or a global corporation. Facilitated by the mission as an ideal as put forward by Peter Drucker, and by vision and values, an inexhaustible universe of tangible personal contributions to shaping reality comes within reach. Cocreation in the character of coevolution gives our work content and meaning; it offers employees a profound experience of being good for someone or something.

In the context of a meaning- and performance-centered corporate culture, shared value can unfold energies through its service to society as a source of meaning in the company, giving the concept of creating shared value extra impact and durability.

Mission, vision, and societal values – catalysts of performance potential

Figure 10. The effect that creating societal value has on employees.

Figure 10 illustrates that in the meaning- and performance-centered approach of the Value Balance in Business, self-actualization by employees need not pose a threat to the company and its performance but can instead be an extraordinary opportunity. If a company is committed to certain value systems through means of a mission and external and internal values, employees realize that they are good for someone or something, that they can bring about something positive, something constructive. The employees thus see that they are involved in shaping reality: this is the most basic form of self-actualization. Gertrud Höhler described this vividly and succinctly: "My goals, your goals, the company's goals: the equation finally adds up."[68]

Throughout the world, "self-realization" has been the major trend of recent decades. The concept of a meaning- and performance-centered corporate culture outlined by the Value Balance in Business gives this new meaning and a new direction—that of collaboration and coevolution. Amazingly, self-realization finds its highest form in service. In the

---

[68] Gertrud Höhler, *Die Sinnmacher: Wer siegen will, muss führen* [The meaning makers: if you want to win, you must lead]. 2nd edition (Berlin: Econ, 2006), 182.

process, individualism is maintained to the extent that each individual can find his or her own meaning, or choose it freely, and then make a decision. In the future, the opportunities a company offers employees to experience meaning will be of critical importance when it comes to competing with other companies. In this regard, let us recall that, according to surveys in 2009, 80–90 percent of all workers in Europe, North America, and Asia expressed a preference for employers who act ethically and in a socially responsible way and are considered to be environmentally friendly.[24] Business is not a parallel world that happens in a vacuum, as the self-serving standard economic model assumes; business life happens in the context of society, and people are not just workers but also citizens and members of a society whom the world of business ultimately serves.

> *Built to Last: Successful Habits of Visionary Companies* by Collins/Porras established that mission, vision, and values *do indeed* have a motivating effect on employees. *Why* this is the case can be understood through meaning-centered psychology, founded by Viktor Frankl and through new insights in the fields of neurobiology and evolutionary biology. These disciplines make an extremely interesting contribution toward understanding the function and operation of corporate cultures and their effect on a company's success. These disciplines are equally important to the specific structuring of corporate cultures in terms of their employees' performance and commitment: only when we know the "why" will we truly be able to realize the potential of a meaning- and performance-centered corporate culture.

4.6 From CSR to CSV—From Cost Factor to Strategic Advantage

As we have shown in detail, the observation that companies that focus on performance for the benefit of customers and society show above-average profitability in the long term can be explained by their being a source of meaning and appreciation for their employees. Employees see that their work is good for someone or something—"I can contribute something valuable to the world; I can make a difference here." They experience recognition and appreciation directly through contact with customers and indirectly through the company's brand and its associated promise of value for its customers (and often also for society). Under these conditions, employees are psychologically willing and able to give their best in their work; for them, it translates into an act of self-realization from which the customers, society, and the shareholders benefit just as much as the employees themselves. Performance-centered, coevolutionary companies are a source of meaning and motivation for their employees.

There is a second important reason for long-term, above-average prosperity of companies that focus on performance: companies that have an awareness of their responsibility toward society are financially compensated in a generous way. Societal values are normative notions of what will provide a positive contribution to society's ability to function. Society rewards this contribution in a way that is economically highly significant for the company. This takes place through both direct and indirect means:

- We have already illustrated the direct route using Ricola as an example: the candies command an attractive price due to the environmentally friendly—and socially useful—cultivation of raw materials that give them an exceptional flavor. The company's business is directly connected with its service to society. This is in line with the basic idea of shared value.
- The indirect route is via reputation: companies that abide by and encourage societal values enjoy trust and prestige with the public; they have a strong reputation. As we shall see, for a company this is key to gaining access to extremely important financial resources.

Both types of resources are much more readily available to performance- and people-oriented companies than to companies that focus on maximizing self-interest.

4.6.1   Creating Shared Value (CSV)

Creating shared value (CSV) is something that those companies that focus on performance and thereby enjoy long-term success, as described by Peters/Waterman, Kotter/Heskett, Collins/Porras, and Joyce/Noriah/Roberson, have actually been practicing all along. Under the banner of their mission, they continue their synergistic interaction with customers *and* society. The mission statements in chapter 4.2 illustrate this. Porter/Kramer have given the concept of shared value an increasingly clear outline and have achieved such a high standing for this through systematic operationalization that creating shared value (CSV) can be considered an independent management discipline on an equal footing with such fields as marketing and HR.

CSV originally has its roots in CSR, corporate social responsibility. However, in terms of effectiveness and efficiency, and thus the generation of benefits for companies and society, it is useful to apply CSR not merely as a public relations or communications tool but to integrate it into the company's core business. Porter/Kramer: "It is not on the margin of what companies do but at the center"[1]—for the following reasons:

-   The company's expertise is greatest in its core business, and it is there where CSR measures are most effective. In other words, it is where they are at their most useful for business and society.[69] If, for example, a globally operating wholesale bank were to spend resources to build wells in Sri Lanka, it would be a far less efficient effort than if they were to engage in a microfinance project.
-   When integrated into a company's core business, cleverly chosen CSR measures can be considered a long-term investment in the company and in society, because they render a return that can bring the company financial benefits directly and not just indirectly via a good reputation. Unlike CSR, CSV is not just a cost to the company—it is an investment; it is concerned with the formation of social capital.

---

[69] See Anker, *Balanced Valuecard*, 112.

– This kind of CSR is transformed into CSV and provides the company with a competitive edge. It also ensures that CSV is not just a fair-weather program that can be discarded as a mere cost factor at the first sign that things are not going well for the company.

Unlike CSR programs, because of its integration into the company's core business, CSV is financially justified and not merely arbitrary. It is also not there to serve a modern-day trade in indulgences with a view to redeeming the company from past or future sins committed in the name of business. With its economic and social importance, CSV belongs within the company's strategy. CSV complies with the idea of cocreation and coevolution. It is exactly for this reason that CSV not only mobilizes forces in the company based on economic considerations but, as a source of meaning, also awakens the employees' motivation and commitment to performance. This is especially true if CSV forms part of a meaning- and performance-centered corporate culture (see fig. 9 and 10).

CSV is an extremely powerful tool for very closely linking together the interests of business and society. The American entrepreneur Paul Polak provides interesting examples in this regard. One such example is his Spring Health project. Around one billion people risk their health every time they drink water. By harnessing the power of market principles, Paul Polak is currently helping to bring clean drinking water to the poorest of the poor in the Indian state of Orissa. Polak has concluded franchise agreements with village kiosks, whereby the kiosk owners receive a three-thousand-liter water tank that they fill themselves. Instead of transporting vast amounts of water, Polak's employees supply the kiosk owners by motorbike with chlorine to disinfect the water. Customers who cannot go to the kiosks themselves get drinking water delivered to their homes for an affordable fee.

According to the German business journal *Brand Eins*,[70] everybody involved receives benefits: The customers get clean water at affordable prices, they maintain their health and creative power, and they do not

---

[70] Thomas Häusler, "Wasser für die Welt" [Water for the world] in *Brand Eins*. http:// www.brandeins.de/archiv/magazin / sinn/artikel/wasser-fuer-die-welt.html, November 17, 2011.

have to spend their money on medication to treat the consequences of using contaminated drinking water. The store owners increase their revenues and income and gain a reputation as a supplier of clean water. Spring Health in turn receives 75 percent of the franchisee's proceeds. Polak is currently working on expanding the Spring Health brand with the concept of flavoring and enriching the drinking water with nutrients. This brings Polak further gains while contributing toward the fight against the widespread malnutrition, especially among children, that remains a problem in developing countries.

Another of Polak's impressive projects is the production of unbeatably priced water pumps (treadle pumps made of bamboo and tin)—affordable to even very poor farmers in Bangladesh. According to *Brand Eins*, many farmers will have tripled their annual income by overcoming their dependence on rainfall, and this also creates new jobs. Polak's organization, IDE (International Development Enterprises), sold two million pumps with the help of a marketing campaign supported by Deza, the Swiss Agency for Development and Cooperation. This allowed for an increased yield on crops to the value of more than one billion euros.

Here is yet another example from India:[71] Nestlé has been transporting milk in the Moga district in a tank truck from a collection point in each village, with the company having fitted out these locations with cooling systems. The same tankers also transport veterinarians, nutritionists, agronomists, quality assurance specialists, and doctors. These professionals bring along medicine for sick animals and offer the farmers monthly training sessions on milk quality assurance through changes to the animals' diets and the methods used for cultivating animal feed. Improved irrigation also plays a role in this context. This has improved the cultivation of rice and grains (i.e., the food supply) and thus in turn benefited the health of the population.

---

[71] Michael E. Porter and Mark R. Kramer, "Strategy & Society. The Link Between Competitive Advantage and Corporate Social Responsibility," *Harvard Business Review* (December 2006). On the same topic, also see Dominic Barton, "Capitalism for the Long Term," *Harvard Business Review* (March 2011) and Valerie Bockstette and Mike Stamp, "Creating Shared Value: A How-to-Guide for the New Corporate (R)evolution", FSG. Source: http://www.fsg.org/.../Creating-Shared-Value-A-How-to-Guide-for-the-New-Corporate-R-evolution.aspx.

Since 1962, the number of milk suppliers has increased from 180 to 75,000 in 650 villages. During this period, the mortality rate of calves has decreased by 75 percent, milk production has increased fifty times, and the quality of the milk has improved. The farmers therefore receive better prices for their milk and, due to regular payments from Nestlé as their consumer, they have become creditworthy. Nestlé itself gains a competitive advantage through raw materials that are of a high quality and delivered reliably. Another advantage for both the farmers and Nestlé is the elimination of the (speculative) middleman, which has made it possible for both sides to base their calculations on stable conditions and thus optimize their investments.

Cisco provides another illustrative example. According to Kathy Mulvany, senior of corporate affairs at Cisco Systems, it was the employees who started the initiative at Cisco. In its early years, Cisco was based in East Palo Alto, California, in what was not exactly the safest area around. Some of Cisco's employees wanted to help the community. There was a school near the Cisco offices, and it was not long before the idea of getting involved there presented itself. "We are a technology company—why not help the school with an Internet connection?" As has so often proved to be the case, it is one thing to introduce technology but quite another for it to be used meaningfully when nobody knows how to use and maintain it. Cisco's employees then came up with the idea of teaching the students how to work with this new technology in a way that is beneficial to them. John Morgridge, former CEO and chairman of the board, liked this idea and took it upon himself to develop the Cisco Networking Academy. Not just the employees but also senior management became involved in the project. This project could not have succeeded without the passion of the company's former and current CEOs—John Morgridge and John Chambers. Chambers was fully convinced of its importance to the company. He is constantly speaking out in favor of investing in society and giving something back to the local communities, especially since it also brings benefits to the company itself.[72]

---

[72] John Kania and Mark Kramer, "Q&A: Roundtable on Shared Value, Executives from 10 major corporations gathered in New York City to discuss the innovative ways that they are putting societal issues at the core of their companies' strategy and operations," *Stanford Social Innovation Review* (Summer 2011). Source: http://www.fsg.org/tabid/191/ArticleId/359/Default.aspx?srpush=true.

Cisco launched its networking academy in 1997 with the aim of assisting schools in getting the most from their networking equipment. Today, more than 900,000 students are trained in the ICT sector annually in over 9,000 academies in 165 countries. Cisco achieves this by collaborating with public and private institutions.

These are some individual examples of the concept of creating shared value in action. If companies consistently lived a meaning- and performance-centered corporate culture, even more could be done in this area in the future.

4.6.2 Reputation—The Company as a "Good Citizen"

Like the standing of a good, trustworthy citizen who lives in accordance with the values of society, a company's good reputation will continue to grow. Such companies become more and more entwined into the social and cultural network of their locations and thus become an increasingly indispensable part of economic, social, and cultural life. This gives them access to many important resources.[73]

What makes a company a "good citizen"? How does it earn a good reputation? And how does this affect the performance, competitive strength, and viability of the company? A mission that is consistently lived, a vision to match, and the kind of values proposed by the shared-value concept all form a good basis for earning a positive reputation. While companies are essentially free to determine the content of their mission, vision, and values, in order to gain the reputation of a "good citizen," they are required to focus on a few specific values—and here,

---

[73] Sulzer, a major corporation based in Winterthur, Switzerland, is an illustrative example. It is a long-established company that has shaped the face of Winterthur in many ways. In 2001, the company experienced a serious crisis: an investor made an attractive offer to the shareholders, but with the likelihood that Sulzer would probably be broken down into component parts and, as a company, would disappear from the scene. The shareholders stood behind the company and did not sell it. Again and again, you could hear the argument: "Sulzer belongs to Winterthur. We cannot allow Sulzer to cease to exist." The trust and loyalty paid off, and Sulzer went on to better times.

too, cocreation and coevolution play a role. Here are some important factors in building a strong reputation:

- *Reliability as an employer*
  The company's treatment of its employees is characterized by recognition and appreciation, with financially driven layoffs a last resort (and not due to short-term cost considerations in the service of profit maximization); the work does not carry a risk of accidents and illnesses; the company supports apprenticeships.

- *Reliability in dealing with the environment*
  The business is environmentally friendly in the way in which it operates and in which employees, their families, and perhaps even customers and shareholders live, even if environmental protection is not—unlike Ricola—part of the company's mission but rather of their CSV.

- *Active cooperation with public institutions*
  Cooperation with training centers, employment offices, health-care services, and institutions with a socially integrative effect, such as cultural and sporting bodies in the areas where the company is located.

- *Refusing to place pressure on authorities and politicians to gain advantages over other companies and institutions that are not based on real achievements*

- *Sensitivity to local cultures*
  Respecting wage structures, leadership styles, content and language of advertising campaigns, and the like.

- *Compliance with existing laws in spirit and meaning (and not just to the letter)*

- *Economic prosperity*

The following points on the positive effects of a good reputation can be found in literature:

- Good standing of the company in the eyes of the public
  - Employer branding: attractiveness as an employer. The best people for the job come knocking at their door, often of their own accord—when competing for talent, this is an important advantage.
  - The public is aware of the company; it is discussed and described in the press in a positive way.
  - Better chances of success in mergers and acquisitions[74]
  - The trust of potential lenders secures financial resources
  - Better access to permits from the government and authorities[75]
  - A good reputation in the media leads to a highly visible presence, which enhances reputation or keeps any scandal within limits when mistakes happen (a good reputation constitutes positive framing, which acts as a "positive bias")
  - A good reputation as a strong brand leads to positive bias in purchasing decisions and confirms to the customer that he or she has made the right decision
- Employees are proud of their company and are actively committed to it; they see it as "theirs" and are willing to share responsibility, for example, when flexibility is needed to handle large orders or when wage concessions are required in times of crisis.
- An appreciative approach to dealing with employees and a focus on performance form a fertile environment for good, constructive agreement between employer and employee representatives.
- A high level of commitment, strong motivation, and a focus on performance make a company fit, flexible, agile, and fast and allow it to focus its energies on the market—it is customer-oriented and competitive.

---

[74] It can be that a company's employees welcome a takeover by another company or a merger because the new partner has a good reputation. On the other hand, a new partner's strong reputation could also instill the fear that the company's culture will be dominated or even completely absorbed.

[75] This is of particular note in Switzerland and other countries with direct democratic instruments.

- This high level of performance correlates with positive customer experiences, which strengthen the company's brand and its competitive standing.
- Success attracts success, and the company's reputation continues to grow.
- Many of these factors are mutually reinforcing.

With regard to CSV and reputation, we can assert the following: companies that through their mission create societal value in addition to economic value are rewarded by the greater social whole in both direct and indirect ways with resources that can be very important financially—resources to which companies that rely only on short-term profit maximization do not have equal access. Just as the meaning-oriented individual can accomplish more than the self-interested *Homo economicus*, the meaning-centered company can achieve more than the self-serving enterprise.

> The quintessence of a meaning- and performance-centered culture: a focus on coevolution benefits a company on two levels. Firstly, offering shared value for the benefit of society provides access to resources that are economically highly interesting. Secondly, the awareness of the interests of society and the reason for the company's existence has a positive effect on the company's sense of meaning and appreciation and consequently on employee motivation and the company's performance. The Value Balance in Business and the concept of creating shared value form a mutually reinforcing system that operates in the interests of customers, employees, shareholders, and society (fig. 11).

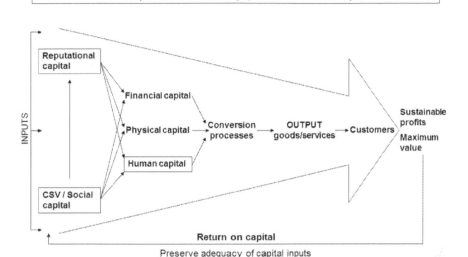

Corporate Stewardship (Value Governance)

(Model: Stephen Young, 2004)

Figure 11. Reputation and shared value can be understood as specific types of capital which, in conjunction with other types of capital, provide a higher return.[76]

4.7 A Company's Internal Culture Shapes Its Look and Its Effect on the Outside World

There are many ways in which a company's culture has an effect on the outside world, and this in turn reverberates internally. In figure 12, the potential inherent in the culture of a "self-transcendent" company is briefly outlined.

Mission, values, and vision are sources of meaning and motivation. When these are lived, every employee can assume that their fellow employees have the same attitude and pursue the same goals. This engenders a team spirit that forms a solid foundation for developing relationships. An environment of mutual trust and respect is created, an environment in which creativity, a spirit of innovation, and constructive, goal-oriented cooperation can flourish.

---

[76] Reference for graph: Stephen Young, *Moral Capitalism: Reconciling Private Interest with the Public Good* (San Francisco: Berrett-Koehler, 2003), 4.

The more open and respectful the dialogue in the company is, and the greater the recognition as an individual, the stronger a sense of commitment will develop among the employees. If people have the freedom to become involved and to participate, they also accept responsibility from the moment they make use of this freedom.

In these companies, everybody is working toward the same goal in a concerted effort so that the recipient of the service can have the best possible solution. When interacting with each other, the stakeholders focus on the matter at hand; disagreements are not personal but deal with the facts of the matter, and people use the opportunity to learn from each other. No valuable energy is wasted on tunnel vision, infighting, power struggles, intrigues, and harassment between individuals and/or departments. The focus is not on a quid pro quo for internal self-centered desires (budget, power, competencies); it is not concerned with glossing over failures or concealing them. Instead, the company's resources can be wholly focused on economic benefits with the precision of a laser beam.

This focus is reflected in the customer's experience; the brand receives a boost and increasingly becomes a promise of performance. Brands build bridges between employees and customers. Within the company, the brand's promise of performance instills a corresponding commitment to customers among the employees and thus becomes an important part of their drive for action and their experience of meaning, as well as being a catalyst for their motivation. Because they have experienced the services associated with the brand, the customers are aware of this internal commitment. They know that the people who work in the company have their customers in mind and are prepared to give them what they want (and more). For their part, the employees are also not focused solely on their products/services but work with the awareness that their customers have expectations that need to be met. This results in a motivational relationship that fosters trust between customers and employees.

At the same time, the employees are going about their work in the knowledge that they are also working toward the benefit of society. In a meaning- and performance-centered corporate culture, customers and society form the *why* and *for whom* for employees, which time and

86

again gives them a sense of worth: "I am needed, what I am doing is important, and what I do has meaning." The energy that is needed to achieve maximum performance is thus freed up, and in the process, so is the ensuing success. This in turn leads to positive feedback with regard to the culture. Experienced as the key to success, it is given the attention that it deserves.

Figure 12 provides a summary of how the culture and market are positively influenced and reinforced in the concept of the Value Balance in Business—under their banner, a company can operate at increasingly higher levels. This brings us back once more to companies that are profitable in the long term—companies that place the emphasis on performance and appreciation for their employees, as we see in the examples from Peters/Waterman, Kotter/Heskett, Collins/Porras, and Joyce/Nohria/Roberson (see chapter 2.2).

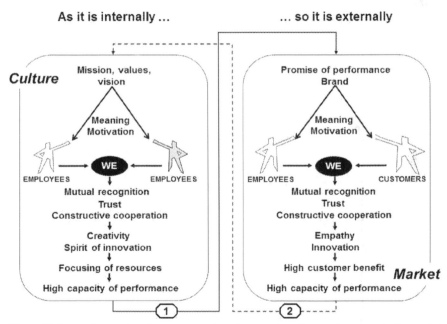

Figure 12. A meaning- and performance-centered corporate culture and success in the market are mutually reinforcing.

The threat to a company that has enjoyed a prolonged streak of success due to its culture does not usually arise through external circumstances but through dangers of its own making: the most fatal mistake is sacrificing a long-term focus on performance for the sake of short-term profits.[77]

4.8 Internal Communication as a Facilitator of Meaning and Recognition

In a meaning- and performance-oriented corporate culture that the Value Balance in Business represents, communication is based on a foundation of mission, vision, and values in the service of meaning; recognition of the individual; and participation—all key factors to ensure that a company's employees feel at home and are willing and able to give their best for the business.

Many communications managers believe their primary function is to communicate. However, designing and ensuring processes within the company, both top down and bottom up, as well as across the boundaries of business units to allow for mutual exchange in the spirit of true participation is nevertheless of much greater significance than the continuous development and dissemination of information from the top down. The goal is for all interaction partners to be in a position to know and understand each other's intentions and motives and to share their expertise. Ultimately, internal communication serves mutual understanding and cooperation toward common goals.

Besides communicating content, this structuring of communication always involves an important aspect of meta-communication: it gives employees the experience of being individually addressed and recognized by management as a fundamental experience of meaning. The sense of "We are down here—you are up there" that often exists can thus be transformed into a unified "we."

It is extremely important that this "we" exists, especially in times of crises. This is possible when management communicates openly, addresses the concerns of employees, and is not above asking them for advice.

---

[77] Jim Collins, *How the Mighty Fall: And Why Some Companies Never Give In* (New York: Harper Collins Publishers, 2009).

By consulting their employees, a European household appliance manufacturer succeeded in increasing its productivity in manufacturing appliances by 13 percent in one year. The productivity in the service area actually increased more and more. Initiatives such as these can lead to an extraordinary increase in employee commitment; processes run more smoothly thanks to the employees, and the staff also feels highly valued.

4.9   Task Design as an Additional Source of Meaning

Meaning in an employee's work comes from the relation that the task has with the company's mission, vision, and values and from the way the specific actions of individual employees are integrated into larger contexts (i.e., job design). We will not pursue this aspect of meaning in detail, but it is worth taking a brief look at some important ideas on the subject.

In this regard, Reinhard Sprenger makes the following suggestions:[78]

- Coherence of planning and execution
- Creative activities that allow people's creative potential to come to the fore (people want to change themselves and their environment through their work)
- Productive activities (the most favorable possible relationship between energy spent and energy produced)
- Interactive activities (be noticed, exchange)

Under the maxim "challenge through meaning," Walter Böckmann makes several suggestions on how to proceed:[79]

- In management, always lead the individual, even if he or she is a member of a group.

---

[78] Reinhard K. Sprenger, *Mythos Motivation: Wege aus einer Sackgasse* [The motivation of myth: a way out of a dead-end street]. 16th edition (Frankfurt/New York: Campus, 1999).

[79] Walter Böckmann, *Sinnorientierte Führung als Kunst der Motivation* [Meaning-oriented management and the art of motivation]. Landsberg/Lech: Verlag Moderne Industrie, 1987, 41.

- Groups must be small, and members must be able to feel that they are part of a group.
- Leadership is neither a "one-size-fits-all" product nor an "off-the-peg" solution but rather a tailor-made approach.
- Anybody who wants to offer meaning must first get to know the expectations that those entrusted to him or her have of meaning, "and that means you must know a whole lot more about your staff, colleagues, or friends than what the often quite superficial interactions at work allow for."

Malik also gives his opinion on this issue, at times under the theme of "providing tasks":[80]

- "People develop themselves with and through their tasks. ... The focus must be on the opportunity to provide a service and to be responsible for it. The service has to be a challenge for the person; he/she should thus, figuratively speaking, become one size bigger than before."
- Put people to work where they already know something, where their strengths and functions are tapped into as much as possible; one should know their weaknesses so as not to put them in situations where their weaknesses will come to the fore.
- There is no correlation between "like to do" and "do well," but there is a correlation between "do easily" and "do well"; there is a danger that we overlook what one does easily exactly because it is easy for him or her.

Can one also experience meaning in monotonous work?

Experiencing meaning is indeed also possible when performing monotonous tasks. A qualitative study by Jesper Isaksen[81] revealed the following as potential sources of meaning:

---

[80] Fredmund Malik, *Führen, Leisten, Leben: Wirksames Management für eine neue Zeit* [Managing, performing, living: effective management for a new era]. 10th edition (Stuttgart: DVA, 2001).
[81] Jesper Isaksen, "Constructing Meaning Despite the Drudgery of Repetitive Work," *Journal of Humanistic Psychology* 40 (2000): 84–107.

- The knowledge that their own contribution is important to the smooth functioning of operational procedures; the key is that their own actions are integrated into larger and therefore meaningful contexts of activity and interdependencies.
- Life within social relationships: the experience of team spirit, mutual responsiveness to professional and personal concerns (see Joachim Bauer, chapter 3.6); here the key is recognition as a person.
- Integration of work in fundamental life contexts, such as gainful employment to support the family.

5. Concepts of Humanity and Company Structuring

If you can find a way to use your signature
strengths at work often, and you also
see your work as contributing to the
greater good, you have a calling. Your
job is transformed from a burdensome
means into a gratification.
　　　　　　　　　　—Martin Seligman

People or employees are managed in relation to how they are viewed, and this is also how structures and organizations are built around them. These are clearly different in their design and in their efficiency and effectiveness, depending on the concept of humanity and the motivation theory on which they are based. When choosing a certain concept of humanity or a particular motivation theory, corporate managers make a preliminary decision, the full extent of which is not always evident to them. Edgar Schein highlights this:

> Managers who assume that people are basically lazy and passive and not interested in the company but only in their own affairs produce companies that become self-fulfilling prophecies. Such managers teach their employees to be lazy and selfish. These circumstances could then be seen as evidence of their original assumptions about human nature. The control-oriented organizations that result from this approach may very well remain in stable positions and stay afloat or even prosper; however, as soon as their environment becomes unstable they go under.[82]

---

[82] Edgar H. Schein, *Organizational Culture and Leadership*, 3rd edition (San Francisco: Jossey-Bass, 2004), 396.

This is a striking example of a self-fulfilling prophecy. The results of the Gallup Engagement Index (see chapter 3.1) are one reflection of this phenomenon.

Anna Maria Pircher-Friedrich generalizes this mechanism: "You condition people through your views, mental models, through the image you have of them."[83]

Managers ultimately create their own human environment in accordance with the image they have of people. This flows into the corporate culture and corporate structuring, and these elements in turn have a selective effect on employees. In the long run, people do not stay in cultures and systems that are not a good match for them, which do not give them a proper feeling of being at home; they physically leave the company, or they distance themselves from it internally, or they get sick.[84]

Over the years, a list of ideas about the nature of human beings has started to emerge from discussions with managers; this list indicates that self-fulfilling prophecies, like those that Edgar Schein describes, are still highly virulent. Statements such as these are still widespread among executives:

People are primarily self-serving:

- — Mankind is selfish by nature; we think only of our own advantage; and the human being is a notorious egotist.
- — The human being is an intelligent animal, selfish and yet smart.
- — The human being is determined only by its instincts.
- — Mankind has no other aim than to pass on its genes.
- — People are inherently aggressive.

---

[83] Anna Maria Pircher-Friedrich, *Mit Sinn zum nachhaltigen Erfolg: Anleitung zur werte- und wertorientierten Führung* [With meaning toward sustainable success: a guide to value and value-based management]. (Berlin: Erich Schmidt Verlag, 2005), 78.
[84] This may also revert to the respective managers themselves. A practical example of this is that managers who see and manage their employees first and foremost as intelligent and cunning animals will cast themselves in the role of tamer—and leave themselves wide open to being attacked from behind by a wild animal. This understanding of leadership is a source of constant stress, aggression, and mutual paralysis.

- Survival of the fittest.
- Ultimately people are governed only by the law of the jungle.
- Human beings are by nature slow, minimalist creatures; you have to drive them all the time.
- As human beings, we are ultimately determined only by our feelings; we are not rational beings.
- The only things that drive people are power, success, prestige, and possessions.
- The only thing that drives people is to safeguard our own offspring.

Alternatives to the image of the self-interested human being are also found, but they are rather rare and are—not surprisingly—found especially among managers who see a long-term focus on performance as imperative for their companies:

- Human beings are ambivalent creatures, capable of both selfishness and altruism.
- Our most important guiding force is our conscience.
- People are capable of freedom and responsibility.
- People want to grow, learn, and develop.
- Stages of development as described by Maslow.
- "I believe in the goodness of people."
- "You have to like your employees."

When a manager's approach is based upon these kinds of convictions about people, it becomes a pleasure to be a leader and put oneself at the service of employees' development and growth.

The relationship between motivation theory/concept of humanity and company structuring is shown in table 2. In reality, the positions taken by companies and leaders are not so extreme, but the comparison in table 2 clearly shows the following: Measured against the 6-f-criteria of fit, fast, flexible, focused, friendly (toward its customers), and fulfilling to work for, companies that see their employees as beings with a desire for meaning and recognition are superior to those that see employees as primarily driven by their pursuit of self-interest. Edgar Schein also confirms this in his opening quote (see above). The concept of humanity that a manager chooses is an important precedent to the success or failure of their company and their own careers.

People/employees are only there to maximize self-interest[85]	People/employees are beings with a desire for meaning and recognition
Everybody strives for their own advantage at the expense of all others. There is an atmosphere of aggression and distrust.	There is mutual trust and an attitude of cooperation for common goals.
Command-and-control hierarchy.	Manager as an enabler, participation.
Management hoards information and knowledge.	Information and knowledge flow through the entire company.
Detailed work descriptions/ specifications lead to rigid cooperation and do not make use of employees' potential (the employees are cogwheels in a big machine).	Flexibility in cooperation allows for optimal complementarity and use of specific skills of employees (the employees are a vital part of a living organism).
Employees' focus is limited to their immediate activity.	Employees are aware of the importance of their contribution to the greater whole; they are integrated into the overarching purpose of the company's existence.
People think in terms of interfaces, in terms of differences.	People think in terms of seams, in terms of what they have in common.
The company as a silo (separated divisions): separation prevents cooperation toward the big picture; strictly standardized chains of command.	Management ensures and guides the strategic and critical processes across departments and business units.
Standardization limits scope for action and paralyzes creativity.	Discretionary power creates creativity.

---

[85] Darwinism, social Darwinism (Herbert Spencer), utilitarianism, Taylorism, the human being as instinct-driven stimulus-response system, and so on.

People/employees are only there to maximize self-interest[85]	People/employees are beings with a desire for meaning and recognition
With the company's departments only focused on their own needs, customers can fall into a no-man's land of "organized irresponsibility" between departments.	Customer needs drive the key processes throughout the individual departments and business units.
Structuring, controls, norm-setting ("right/wrong"), standardization, partialization, thinking in terms of coercion, enticement, status, hierarchy, limited action horizon.	Values ("important/unimportant"), meaning, participation, trust, cooperation, broader action horizon, freedom, (self-) responsibility, motivation, performance, orientation to the outside world, thoughts, and actions in shared tasks.
Internal orientation: companies that are fixated on themselves and their own interests.	External orientation: companies that focus on performance to the benefit of their customers and society.
Correlation with companies that focus on maximizing profits.	Correlation with companies that focus on performance.
Extrinsic motivation.	Intrinsic motivation.
Very little room for using own discretion at work is a source of stress and illness[86] that reduces productivity.	More room for using own discretion due to control over own work.
Low ability to adapt, "dinosaurs."	6 f: fit, fast, flexible, friendly (customers), focused (market), fulfilling to work for (employees).

Table 2. Concepts of humanity as determinants of corporate structuring and organization.[87]

[86] Wilkinson and Pickett, *The Spirit Level*, 75.
[87] Anker, "Co-Evolution", 152.

> The concept of humanity with which employees are identified has a direct impact on the management, structuring, and organization of a company, on its adaptability and capacity for performance for the benefit of customers and society, and in turn, on its profitability.

Table 2 once again demonstrates the correlation between the concept of meaning-oriented people/employees and a company with a focus on performance primacy on the one hand and the concept of self-interested people/employees and companies with a focus on maximizing profits on the other hand. One conclusion to be drawn from this is that in the long run, it is not possible for a company to promote a culture of short-term profit maximization internally while projecting a focus on performance primacy to the outside world or vice versa.

Take away: The shared-value approach is not structurally neutral; its effectiveness also depends on the structuring and organization of the companies that pursue this approach. Because of their rigid, relatively poor adaptability and capacity for performance, their inward-oriented structures and their culture of focusing on maximization of self-interest, companies that base their philosophy on the idea that human beings are basically self-interested are not in a position to truly bring to bear the potential for usefulness and success of the concept of shared value. This is only possible if the creation of shared value is embedded in the context of a meaning- and performance-centered corporate culture and a 6-f structure (see fig. 13).

Figure 13 presents the quintessence of the considerations of chapters 3–5. In chapter 3, mankind's existential needs—our desire for meaning and our need for recognition as an individual—are identified. Where these needs are satisfied, we are mentally and psychologically willing and able to do our best. Chapter 4 was dedicated to building these existential needs and the capacity for satisfying them in a meaning- and performance-centered corporate culture—with their main drivers being mission, vision, and values. Chapter 5 briefly considered the relationship between the concept of humanity/meaning- and performance-centered corporate philosophy and culture on the one hand and the appropriate structuring of the company on the other hand. This is the foundation of the Value Balance in Business.

> The relationship between motivation theory/concept of humanity, culture, structure/organization with the capacity for performance and profitability of the company

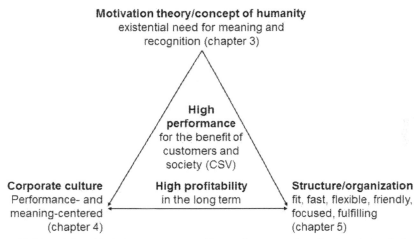

Figure 13. The relationship between concept of humanity, corporate culture, and structuring of the company. These relationships are interdependent.

This brings us to the end of this examination of the Value Balance in Business as the core of a meaning- and performance-centered corporate philosophy and culture. The following chapters are dedicated to outlining a tool for corporate culture audits and assessments based on the Value Balance in Business, which serves in the development of a meaning- and performance-centered corporate culture.

6. The Value Balance in Business[88] as a Tool for Corporate Culture Assessments and Audits—Structure and Contents

Those who look closely and listen
carefully, are better leaders.
                                        —Winfried Prost

6.1 Introduction

We have now identified the essential elements of the Value Balance in Business as a key concept for a meaning- and performance-centered corporate culture:

1. The main target variable is *employee motivation* as the source of the company's potential for achievement.
2. The Value Balance in Business is oriented toward companies that have a *performance primacy* as the basis for long-term, above-average profitability.
3. The company's performance primacy is rooted in its culture in the *mission, vision,* and internal and external *values*—these are the core factors, the focal points of a meaning- and performance-centered corporate culture.
4. The company's ultimate answer to employees' existential need for *meaning* in what they do and *recognition as individuals* lies in its mission, vision, and values.
5. Where the mission, vision, and values are consistently embodied in everyday working life, they become—as a source of meaning

---

[88] The Value Balance in Business is a protected trademark in the United States of America.

and recognition—the fundamental *catalysts* of employees' spiritual *motivation* and psychological *commitment*.

6. Companies with a primacy of performance see their true *reason for existence* as being there to effectively and efficiently *solve problems for customers and society* in their role as a provider of services; a performance primacy is associated with high long-term profitability.

7. The existence of such companies is meaningful not just from the perspective of the company and its customers but also from the perspective of its employees and shareholders. These companies are highly legitimized and occupy a firm place in the economy and society; they are integrated into these institutions, and their relationship is one of intense reciprocal exchange of resources for the benefit of all involved. The basic idea behind it is one of *coevolution*—of mutual service, joint development, and shared growth.

These seven elements form the foundation of the Value Balance in Business as a meaning- and performance-centered approach to corporate culture. It acts as a catalyst for employee commitment and motivation. In doing so, it also frees the energy needed for successfully creating shared value (and this in turn has the effect of an even greater increase in energy in companies with a meaning- and performance-centered corporate culture). Furthermore, the concept that the Value Balance in Business proposes for a corporate culture forms the foundation of culture audits for private and public companies and other institutions with a performance mandate. Its goal is to analyze whether, where in the company, how, and to what extent employee motivation can be enhanced as the company's main source of energy, innovation, and transformation.

6.2 How Value Balance in Business Corporate Culture Audits Are Structured

The key questions at the core of a Value Balance in Business corporate culture audit are as follows:

1. To what extent do employees see meaning in their work?
2. To what extent do they experience recognition as individuals in the company?

3. How pronounced is the resulting motivation on the part of the employees?

From this, it becomes evident that in the Value Balance in Business corporate culture audit, the company is considered from the perspective of the employees, both those in management and those being managed. This is in line with the premise that enhanced value for the company starts with an increase in appreciation for its employees (see chapter 2.5); they are the main source of the company's success, they are behind the 6-f criteria of fit, fast, flexible, focused, friendly, and fulfilling to work for, and ultimately they shape the company's image as a unique entity and provider of quality services.

The Value Balance in Business audit/assessment uses a structured grid to systematically assess the extent to which employees experience meaning and recognition in the company. The idea derives from the Balanced Scorecard, which in strategy development always abides by the same four variables or perspectives to be implemented by the company (the financial perspective, customer perspective, internal processes perspective, and the learning and growth perspective).[89]

The perspectives of the Value Balance in Business corporate culture audits/assessments derive from a consideration of all the areas in the company—again from the perspective of the employees—where sources of meaning and recognition exist or could exist. These are listed below and then explained in more detail:

1. *Leadership* or *senior management*—as those responsible for the corporate culture as a source of motivation for employees and as an independent factor in the company's success
2. *Mission, vision, and values*—the fundamental sources of meaning and recognition in the corporate culture
3. The relationship between employees and *customers*
4. The *employees* themselves and their dispositions

---

[89] Robert S. Kaplan and David P. Norton, *Balanced Scorecard.* (Stuttgart: Schäffer Poeschel, 1997).

5. The attitude employees have toward the company's *products and services*
6. The company's *market position and capacity for innovation* from the employees' point of view
7. The company's *reputation* in society as gauged by the employees
8. The *shareholders* and their attitude toward the company, from the employees' perspective
9. *Internal communications* as assessed by the employees

This is the basic format for all Value Balance in Business audits and assessments. Data is collected in each of these areas through online surveys or printed questionnaires or in group and one-on-one discussions with employees. This broad spectrum of considerations provides the balance in the "Value Balance in Business."

The three core perspectives under consideration are the *customers*, from whom the resources that the company needs for its existence originate, the *employees* (at all levels) as the authors of the company's performance vis-à-vis the customers, and the *shareholders*, who make available the resources that a company requires for its development. From the perspective of the Value Balance in Business, management is the company's supreme servant—the management team carries the company. In other words, it does everything that is needed for the company to fulfill its purpose. The company's performance is measured by a long-term increase in its value, and this is the result of the work performed by both the management team and the other employees.

We are not alone in our service-oriented approach toward the company; there are empirical studies that also indicate that it is a reliable means for executives and their companies to achieve success. According to Collins, individuals in management who have succeeded in leading their companies to consistently higher prosperity—Collins calls them "Level 5 leaders"—are characterized as follows:

> Level 5 leaders channel their ego needs away from themselves and into the larger goal of building a great company. It's not that Level 5 leaders have no ego or self-interest. Indeed, they are incredibly ambitious—*but*

their ambition is first and foremost for the institution, not themselves.[90]

The capacity successful leaders have for self-distancing and self-transcendence are clearly expressed here.

In this context, it is also worth considering what Malik has to say on the topic of "effective managers":

Rank, status and privileges are not important to them per se; they are important to them only insofar as they assist them in making a specific contribution.[91]

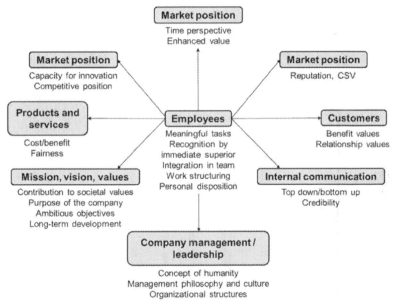

The nine perspectives of the *Value Balance in Business* audit

Figure 14. The nine perspectives of the Value Balance in Business audit with their most important aspects of meaning and recognition.

---

[90] Jim Collins, *Good to Great: Why Some Companies Make the Leap and Others Don't* (New York: Harper Business, 2001), 21.
[91] Malik, *Führen, Leisten, Leben,* 89.

Kotter/Heskett comment on the other end of the spectrum as follows: "At the lower-performing firms, managers seemed to care more about either their own careers or perks or specific products and technologies."[92]

With its nine dimensions, the Value Balance in Business audit is clearly much more diverse (i.e., more nuanced) than most audits of a similar kind. This is in particular due to the inclusion of Perspective 2 (mission, vision, and values), Perspective 3 (customers), Perspective 5 (products and services), Perspective 6 (market position and innovation), and Perspective 8 (shareholders). With this diversity of perspectives, the Value Balance in Business audit embraces a variety of possible sources of meaning and provides several different measures for increasing employee motivation. You could say that this follows the old physician's rule that the treatment can only be as good as the diagnosis.

6.3 The Nine Perspectives of the Value Balance in Business Audit and the Meaning They Embody as Sources of Motivation for Employees

The individual perspectives in terms of meaning and recognition—still from the point of view of employees—will now be explained briefly. These perspectives are specified and operationalized in more detail in the tables that follow. We will approach this in two stages: the various aspects of meaning will be presented in the first stage (the purpose of our actions, recognition as a reason for being), while the second stage comprises the assessment aspects. These reflect the content of questions to employees in a summarized form. This then results in a list of questions that are given to employees of all levels, which can be used for audits, assessments, and self-assessments in companies or sections within companies. It should be noted that "companies" here refers to all institutions—both private and public—with a performance mandate.

---

[92] John P. Kotter and James L. Heskett, *Corporate Culture and Performance* (New York: The Free Press, 1992), 52.

6.3.1   Perspective 1: Leadership/Senior Management

One of the main tasks of management is to develop and maintain the culture, especially with regard to mission, vision, and values. This includes determining the concept of humanity that the company has adopted. Depending on this view, a company's management team will lean either more toward being a command-and-control body or toward being an empowerer of employees that enables them to work independently (i.e., taking a leadership role), thereby also characterizing the structure and organization of the company (see chapter 5).

Looking at the aspect of the perception of meaning, the question is raised of how well the management team is able to communicate the company's goals and demonstrate to employees what they (the employees) contribute toward achieving objectives. Under the aspect of recognition, topics such as the management team's willingness to engage in dialogue—in other words, their receptiveness to the concerns of the employees—are addressed. This last point is an important factor for the faith employees have in their management team. The greater the employees' faith, the more positively they see the future of the company, and the more meaningful it will be from their perspective to give their best in working for the company. Other points that are included under the heading "Leadership/Senior Management" are the employees' commitment to the company and their motivation—which, to some extent, is the result of all the preceding factors.

Aspects of meaning	Assessment aspects (perception and assessment by employees)
1. Meaning of tasks	• Employees are familiar with the company's most important objectives • Employees know how they can contribute to achieving company objectives • General feeling of meaning in their work

Aspects of meaning	Assessment aspects (perception and assessment by employees)
2. Recognition (reason for being)	• Senior management's degree of interest in the employees and their concerns • Extent of the respect of senior management toward employees as individuals, not just as workers
3. The company's competitiveness in general	• The company's degree of competitiveness (market-driven offerings, innovation)
4. Future prospects	• The company's prospects for the future • Thinking in terms of opportunities instead of in terms of problems
5. Communication (information and how this is meaningfully organized, participation)	• In matters that are important in the company, employees know what these mean for them specifically; openness of communication • Information flow/exchange between the business units
6. Context of the work	• Quality of the working environment/extent to which employees feel at home in the company • The level of mutual trust in the company in general • Overall functioning of processes (how smoothly do processes run in the company in general?)
7. Confidence in senior management	• Degree of confidence in senior management • Senior management manages linearly and consistently • Senior management places the interests of the company before their own
8. Loyalty to the company	• Degree of loyalty employees have toward the company
9. Willingness	• Level of motivation toward the company • General personal performance in carrying out professional tasks
10. Satisfaction	• Overall satisfaction

Aspects of meaning	Assessment aspects (perception and assessment by employees)
11. Change processes (optional)	• Perception of a current or forthcoming change process as either an opportunity or a threat • Job security

Table 3. Items for Perspective 1: Leadership/Senior Management.

6.3.2 Perspective 2: Mission, Vision, and Values

This topic does not need further explanation here; it suffices to say that questions along the following lines are important for the audit: Does the company make any statement that could be classified under mission, vision, and values? How widely are these known in the company? How consistently are they adhered to? If none of the available information or documents gives a clear picture, it is best to research value statements in discussions before the actual survey.

Asking to what extent a senior management team is a role model for the rest of the employees in terms of adhering to the mission, vision, and values addresses one aspect of leadership. If the management team leads by example, they are entitled to consistently demand that the rest of the employees adhere to the company's mission, vision, and values too.

Aspects of meaning	Assessment aspects (perception and assessment by employees)
1. Mission	• Existence/visibility in the company • General presence in the company/frequency of addressing this topic • Importance in day-to-day work • Effect on motivation/degree of enthusiasm
2. Vision	• Existence/visibility in the company • General presence in the company/frequency of addressing this topic • Importance in day-to-day work • Effect on motivation/degree of enthusiasm

Aspects of meaning	Assessment aspects (perception and assessment by employees)
3. Internal values	• Existence/visibility in the company • General presence in the company/frequency of addressing this topic • Importance in day-to-day work/degree of commitment
4. External values: Relationship values	• Existence/visibility in the company • Importance in day-to-day work/degree of commitment
5. External values: Utility values	• Existence/visibility in the company • General presence in the company/frequency of addressing this topic
6. Role models	• Employees' perception of the degree of commitment of the managers responsible for these values

Table 4. Items for Perspective 2: Mission, Vision, and Values.

6.3.3 Perspective 3: Customers and Perspective 5: Products And Services

From the perspective of the employees, there are important questions of meaning and recognition that relate to the customers. In terms of utility values, the significant question for employees is whether they are in a position to adequately solve the customers' problems—in other words, whether they can be good for someone or something. In terms of relationship values, for the employees as beings capable of empathy, the question is whether they have the material resources and knowledge to work with the customers in a manner that they themselves would like to be served if they were in the customers' position. More specifically, do employees have the freedom to advise customers to the best of their knowledge and belief, or are they being asked to maximize revenue per customer (in other words, to persuade them to buy things they do not really want)? Depending on this, employees and customers experience the human relationship as either more or less motivating. From the perspective of meaning, recognition, and performance, the question is then to what extent are employees who do not have contact with customers aware of the customers' needs, and do they know how to best support their colleagues who work in sales, marketing, and customer care?

Aspects of meaning	Assessment aspects (perception and assessment by employees)
1. Customer satisfaction	• Overall satisfaction of customers with the company and its services (as perceived by employees)
2. Products and services	• Extent of the benefits of the product(s) or services rendered to customers; appropriateness of the cost/benefit and cost/performance ratios (in the perception of the employees)
3. Contact with customers	• Assessment of the available resources and expertise to create optimal customer contact (from the perspective of the employees)
4. Customer presence	• Extent to which customers and their needs are of importance among employees, even if they have no direct customer contact (self-assessment)

Table 5. Items for Perspectives 3 (Customers); and 5 (Products and Services).

The above table on Perspective 3 also contains items on Perspective 5: Products and Services. These perspectives can be provided separately if needed; here, they are combined for ease of use in the survey.

6.3.4   Perspective 4: Employees

Some general aspects of personnel management have already been covered in Perspective 1. In Perspective 4, the focus is therefore on direct management relationships—in other words, on the relationship between employees and their immediate supervisors. Other points of interest are work structuring, team integration, and issues concerning human resources management in the narrower sense, such as compensation and benefits, training, promotion practices, resources available in the workplace, and so on.

The second part of Perspective 4, the employees' individual dispositions is an important consideration. So, too, is the importance that they assign to work in their lives, their problem-solving behaviors, coping skills (i.e., their ability to deal with stress, failure, and conflict in a constructive way), their capacity for teamwork, their performance orientation, the importance of material motivation, and the degree of intangible motivation, as well as their receptiveness for new ideas. This all forms part of self-assessment.

Aspects of meaning	Assessment aspects	Topics for possible questions
1. Leadership by direct supervisors (management styles and leadership qualities)	• Understanding of motives and intentions	• Supervisors seek the opinion of employees
	• Joint action with the employees	• Supervisors support employees in difficult situations
	• Emotional resonance with employees	• Employees are responded to in an emotionally appropriate way[93]
	• Mutual attention	• Joint goal setting • Employees know why and for whom they carry out their tasks
	• Recognition for employees	• Employees feel acknowledged as individuals • Employees receive regular feedback from supervisors
	• Loyalty	• Loyalty to employees
	• Expertise	• Supervisors' expertise

---

[93] "Resonance will not be forced, but in a relationship—of any kind—it is an eminently unifying, highly motivating element." See Bauer, Prinzip *Menschlichkeit*, 192.

Aspects of meaning	Assessment aspects	Topics for possible questions
2. Work structuring	• Work content	• Diversity, variety
	• Self-realization	• Degree of applicability of own knowledge and their own skills at work
	• Empowerment	• Opportunities for personal development in tasks
3. Team integration	• Integration	• How comprehensively employees are able to integrate in their team(s)
	• Recognition	• Extent to which they take a serious interest in each other, mutual respect • Concern for welfare of colleagues • Striving for trustworthiness
	• Humor	• Hearty laugher is a frequent occurrence in the team
4. Team-orientation	• Cooperation	• I am a team motivator • Team success over personal success • I promote teamwork • Personal importance of teamwork
5. Personnel management in the narrower sense	• Compensation and benefits	• Satisfaction with compensation package • Assessment of variable salary component
	• Career opportunities	• Prospects for promotion for people who are good at their jobs • Fairness of the promotion system

Aspects of meaning	Assessment aspects	Topics for possible questions
	• Opportunities for continuing education	• Impact on the position of employees in the labor market
	• Work equipment	• I possess all of the necessary equipment in order to fulfill the tasks correctly
6. Personal employee dispositions	• Initiative	• Degree of personal drive, on own initiative
	• Openness to new ideas	• Openness to new ideas, new ways of doing things
	• Willingness to take risks	• Willingness to break new ground, even if this is associated with risk
	• Coping skills	• Ability to tolerate uncertainty • Coping with failure

Table 6. Items for Perspective 4: Employees.

Looking at the aspect of meaning and recognition, the important question is whether employees believe in your company's products, whether they are convinced that the customers are getting a reasonable benefit for the price they are paying, and whether the company is fair. The sooner this becomes the case, and the more the employees are in a position to have faith in the company's products and see its dealings with customers as fair, the greater the enthusiasm with which they deal with the customers, and, usually, the greater the sales success.

The question topics for Perspective 5 (Products and Services) are listed together with those for Perspective 3: Customers.

6.3.5 Perspective 6: The Company's Market Position and Capacity for Innovation

The more positively employees assess the position of their company's products in the market—the more they are convinced that they are working with an innovative company that keeps up with developments or is actually at the top of its game and sets standards—the more positively they see the future of the company, and the more it makes sense for them to commit to the company and maintain or strengthen their faith in it.[94]

A company's standing in its industry is an important source of recognition for its employees; it makes a difference whether at conferences and trade fairs you can meet the competitors' employees on an equal footing or whether you want to avoid them.

Aspects of meaning	Assessment aspects (perception and assessment by employees)
1. Competitiveness of the company	• Assess the company's competitiveness in the industry
2. Innovation	• With regard to the level of development of its products, does the company count among the leading companies that help determine the market, or is it a follower? • Importance of belonging to a leading company from the perspective of the employees
3. Image/reputation of the products and services	• Assessment of the reputation of the products and/or services in the market

Table 7. Items for Perspective 6: The company's market position and capacity for innovation.

---

[94] Under the banner of short-term maximization of profit, it is often the case that companies report top results but announce redundancies at the same time. The corresponding signals that reach the employees are fatal, and the damage to the company is serious; what started out as motivational forces turn into fear and become negative motivators. In the long run, this can paralyze both people and companies.

6.3.6 Perspective 7: The Company's Reputation in Society

In terms of meaning and recognition as well as employees' personal prestige, it is important to note whether a company has such a good public reputation that its employees are proud of being associated with it and find pleasure in belonging to the company. An indication of this is whether the employees speak of "we" when they mean the company. In these circumstances, they consider the business as their own and feel jointly responsible for it—which is a fundamental requirement for a 6-f-business. This has clear consequences for employee motivation.

Aspects of meaning	Assessment aspects (perception and assessment by employees)
1. General image of the reputation of the company	• Assessment of the degree of support among the public • The degree of willingness to recommend the company as an employer to their peers • Willingness to admit to being part of the company, pride in the company
2. Reliability as an employer	• Assessment of how employees are dealt with in general/appreciation for employees • Degree of protection against occupational accidents and illnesses • The degree of prudence in hiring/dismissal
3. Reliability in dealing with the environment	• Environmental impact of production • Environmental impact of products and services
4. Respecting local cultures	• The degree to which the company takes local economic, social, and cultural factors into consideration (wage policy; respect for norms, customs, and practices; how they present themselves in public, speech, images, etc.)

Table 8. Items for assessing the company's reputation from the perspective of employees.

6.3.7 Perspective 8: Shareholders

In terms of aspects of meaning, to the employees, it is important whether the shareholders believe in the concept of companies with a performance primacy and pursue a long-term perspective or whether they are merely owners whose objective for the company is to make money quickly and then withdraw their returns as soon as possible or sell off the company in its individual parts. Once this impression takes hold in a company, employee motivation collapses; employees no longer see any sense in giving this company their all.

Aspects of meaning	Assessment aspects (perception and assessment by employees)
1. The company's prosperity	• I look forward to the future with optimism, because my company is vigorous, dynamic, and constantly evolving
2. Long-term perspective	• To the owners, it is more important that the company exists for as long as possible and is steadily successful than to achieve the maximum profit in the shortest possible time
3. Balance between economy and society	• The shareholders are not merely concerned with money; they also acknowledge that their company has a social responsibility

Table 9. Items relating to shareholders.

6.3.8 Perspective 9: Internal Communication

The central role of internal communication is to help employees obtain the information and knowledge that would enable them to:

1. Properly understand the events in and around the company and position themselves within these in a meaningful manner in order to act appropriately
2. Perceive their tasks as effectively and efficiently as possible
3. Apply their knowledge and experience and take part in the information exchange

As mentioned in chapter 4.8, communication that is designed in this way includes the dimension of meaning and appreciation for the individual.

Aspects of meaning	Assessment aspects (perception and assessment by employees)
1. General willingness to communicate	• The supervisor's door is open for employees
2. Feedback on suggestions for improvements	• Regularity and substance of responses to suggestions from employees
3. Information on the company's performance	• Quality and frequency of information about important issues for the employees' organizational units (achievement of objectives, restructuring, personnel issues, financial success, etc.) and the company as a whole
4. Quality of information flow within the company	• Information flows to the places where it is needed (no monopolizing) • Employees are equipped with the information they need to perform their tasks
5. Credibility	• Management keeps everybody informed openly and honestly
6. Optional aspects in change processes	• Clarity and usefulness of information from management about change processes for employees • Opportunity for employees to participate with company management in change processes

Table 10. Items on Perspective 9: Communication.

6.4 The Variable of "Motivation"

The Value Balance in Business audit operates with three indicators to define and capture employee motivation. Questions that are asked pertain to motivation to work for the company, personal performance orientation, and emotional commitment to the company (see table 3, chapter 6.3.1). These three indicators are combined unweighted in the "motivation" index variable.

7. The Value Balance In Business in Action— A Look at the Audit in Practice

Regardless of technologies, a company must maintain its own culture, which is based primarily on human targets.
      —Irene Kärcher, former entrepreneur

7.1   Introduction

Data is collected for the Value Balance in Business audit in a structured way, corresponding to the nine perspectives laid out in the previous chapter. The questionnaire is comprehensive, and when it is presented to the employees in its entirety, completing it requires some effort. If the audit is supported by good communication—making the objectives known to everybody so that the process is meaningful—this does help to overcome motivational obstacles. It is not always essential for all the questions to be asked during a Value Balance in Business audit; nevertheless, it is recommended that all nine perspectives be taken into consideration. Qualitative preliminary studies usually offer a good indication of which areas require in-depth probing and which areas may be assessed in less detail. In other words, the Value Balance in Business questionnaire lends itself to flexible application. This is particularly due to the fact that the Value Balance in Business does not pursue an external benchmark as its primary goal but instead considers each company as a unique entity. A company's corporate culture is the bearer of its spirit; it is what makes a company unique. From this perspective, in the area of corporate culture, an external benchmark would be a contradiction in terms. This is because it evens out differences instead of encouraging them (the key being "differentiation"), especially if developments in the corporate culture have been initiated in line with a philosophy of best practices.

Working with the full list of questions outlined in the previous chapter or with a shortened version will provide a substantial amount of data to work with. The two most important data-reduction processes in the Value Balance in Business audit are factor analysis and cluster analysis, with the main focus being on factor analysis (see fig. 15). The second important step in implementing the model is a multiple regression of the factors that influence motivation, which is the most important target variable in the Value Balance in Business corporate culture concept and audit. This method enables us to establish what the impact of each of these factors is on employee motivation individually and to what degree motivation is affected by these factors overall—which is extremely important information for deciding on actions to be taken with regard to corporate development.

The degree of detail and differentiation in the results of a corporate culture audit are determined by the client's needs. The method used for collecting data will also depend on whether an audit is intended to provide an overview of a company's culture and its associated performance potential or whether in-depth and comprehensive corporate culture development is planned. The time needed to conduct the audit will vary accordingly. The standard approach to Value Balance in Business audits is the use of online surveys.

The following chapters present different facets of a specific Value Balance in Business audit (for a medium-sized European company), conducted by means of a comprehensive online survey. They offer some ideas and further information on possible applications for Value Balance in Business audits.

Structure of the *Value Balance in Business* corporate culture audit

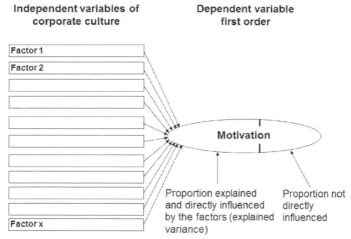

Figure 15. The model for the Value Balance in Business audit. This is based on factor analysis and multiple regression of the factors that influence the variable "motivation."

7.2 Motivation—The Primary Target Value of the Value Balance in Business

Grouping of employees by their degree of motivation
(average motivation in the company: 8.3 on a scale with 1 = lowest rating and 10 = highest rating)

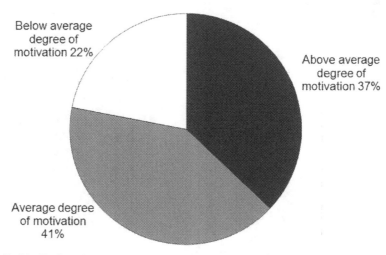

Figure 16. Distribution of motivation within the company (n = 425).

As noted in chapter 6.4, the variable "motivation" is an index variable consisting of three different survey items: motivation to work for the particular employer as a company, personal motivation ("work ethic"), and emotional attachment to the company.

On a scale where 1 = minimum score and 10 = maximum score, an average score for motivation of 8.3 was determined for this company, based on the index variable.

An initial rough analysis (fig. 16) shows that about three-quarters (74 percent) of all employees of this company express at least an average degree of motivation, while more than one-third of all collaborators (37 percent) is actually motivated above average. Measured against the international average, which indicates that 80 percent of all employees have only a weak or no emotional relationship at all with their employer, the situation in the company presented here is very different. The areas where untapped potential exists in the company will be revealed in the course of our analysis.

The next step is to look at how motivation is distributed within the company (fig. 17).

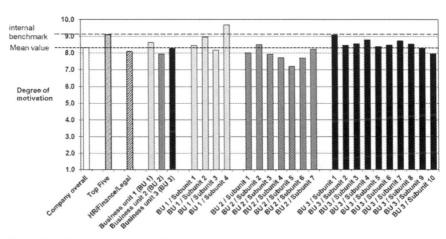

Figure 17. Distribution of motivation within the company (n = 425).

Working on a 10-point scale, the empiric evidence points to a rather skewed distribution, with most of the responses in the range from 5 to 9. The spread of motivation by business units (BU) and their subunits is comparatively low. Nevertheless, at the 95 percent confidence level, the difference between the motivation in business unit 1 (BU 1) and business unit 2 is significant. It is already evident from this graph that the individual subunits of business unit 2 nevertheless vary considerably in terms of their motivation and thus require differentiated initiatives to improve performance.

In this company, it is of concern that the areas of activity that are directly grouped around the management structure and whose function it is to provide support services—HR, finance, legal—show below average scores for motivation. This means that the experts at the corporate executive level have a more negative view of the company's future prospects than the rest of the employees. Here it would be important to find out what signals are emanating from the management environment and spreading through to the rest of the company. It would be particularly problematic if these signals were to contradict communication from management.

To develop the different business units toward the top five in terms of their motivation is a real challenge, but the top five provide valuable information and ideas as to what initiatives should be implemented where. Given the strong differences in motivation between the subunits, an external benchmark would be far too general and not very helpful; in an attempt to increase motivation, it could very well end up pointing the process in the wrong direction.

7.3 Doing the Right Things Right—Finding an Effective Lever

Factor analysis is a mathematical tool to identify topics that belong together; these are derived from the employees' viewpoint and are based on their response behavior in surveys. In other words, factor analysis is used to generate thematic areas. These thematic areas provide important clues as to the perspective from which employees see (and therefore evaluate) their company. By grouping individual topics under thematic areas, a superordinate structure is created.

In the example used here, ten factors with a total of twenty-seven assessment aspects (see chapter 6) proved to be an optimal solution. Table 11 indicates which assessment aspects were summarized in factors and how they were described. Based on how each item was scored by the employees, it was possible to determine a score for each factor.

Factor description	Mean value of factor[95]	Assessment aspects/Key Performance Indicators (KPIs)
1. Recognition as an individual	7.3	• Respecting employees as individuals • Quality of the work climate
2. Values	8.7	• Striving for credibility with colleagues • Concern for the welfare of colleagues • Environmental protection
3. Customers	7.9	• Degree to which customers and their needs are important to employees, even if they have no direct customer contact (self-assessment) • Assessment of the company's competitiveness in the industry • Customer-related values
4. Market position	7.2	• Company's status as a leading company with regard to the level of development of its products and services • Importance of being a leading company from the perspective of the employees • Assessment of the reputation of the products in the home market
5. Coping skills	7.9	• Ability to tolerate uncertainty • Coping with failure
6. Teamwork	8.2	• I am a motivator • Team success over personal success • Attitude toward teamwork

---

[95] Rating scale 1 ("Do not agree at all") to 10 ("Agree completely").

Factor description	Mean value of factor[95]	Assessment aspects/Key Performance Indicators (KPIs)
7. Company	7.5	• Company's future prospects • Mission elicits enthusiasm[96] • Company as industry leader • Proud of the company
8. Compensation	6.9	• Satisfaction with the company's compensation package
9. Team leadership	8.0	• Supervisors seek the opinion of employees • Supervisors support employees, especially in difficult situations • Loyalty toward employees • Employees feel acknowledged as individuals
10. Innovation	8.5	• Openness to new ideas • Willingness to take risks

Table 11. Factors and their underlying assessment aspects.

With the focus of the Value Balance in Business on a meaning- and performance-centered corporate culture, the next and ultimately crucial step lies in answering these questions: How do these factors affect employee motivation? How strong is the impact of each individual factor on motivation, and to what degree can this be actively developed? The answer to these questions lies in a multiple (in this case, linear) regression of these ten factors that influence the index variable "motivation" (see fig. 18).

Seven of these ten factors have a directly discernible effect on employee motivation in this company. Their influence on motivation is substantial; with their help, motivation can be directly influenced by over 60 percent.

Statistically, the factors "Compensation," "Team Leadership," and "Innovation" have no direct effect on motivation in this company.

---

[96] A provisional mission statement was used for testing purposes; a real mission was not available at the time of the survey.

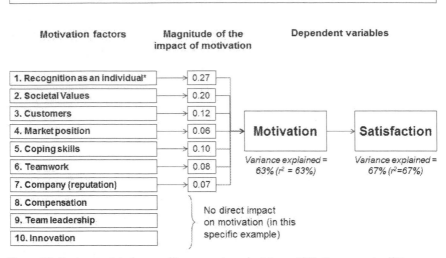

Specific example of a factor model of motivation

Motivation factors	Magnitude of the impact of motivation	Dependent variables

1. Recognition as an individual* → 0.27
2. Societal Values → 0.20
3. Customers → 0.12
4. Market position → 0.06
5. Coping skills → 0.10
6. Teamwork → 0.08
7. Company (reputation) → 0.07

Motivation → **Satisfaction**

Variance explained = 63% (r^2 = 63%)   Variance explained = 67% (r^2=67%)

8. Compensation
9. Team leadership
10. Innovation

No direct impact on motivation (in this specific example)

Figure 18. Factor model of a specific research project (n = 425). For example, if the score for factor 1 ("Recognition as an individual") increases by one point, motivation increases by 0.27 points.

In this company, at least, our hypothesis is confirmed that satisfaction is not a prerequisite for high performance; on the contrary, satisfaction results when employees experience that they can provide products or services that are good for someone or something—that they have meaning. In this company, satisfaction increases slightly disproportionately as a function of motivation; if the latter increases by one point, the former increases by as much as 1.13 points.

Given the significant influence of seven of the ten factors on the level of employee motivation (variance covered: 63 percent), one can draw the conclusion that it would pay for this company to address the topic of motivation in more depth. The most effective levers in this case, which should be given particular attention, can be deduced from the relative influence each factor has on motivation in the company.

7.4   Tailored Data Processing

The impact the individual factors have on employee motivation and how the employees score these factors can be represented in a fourfold table.

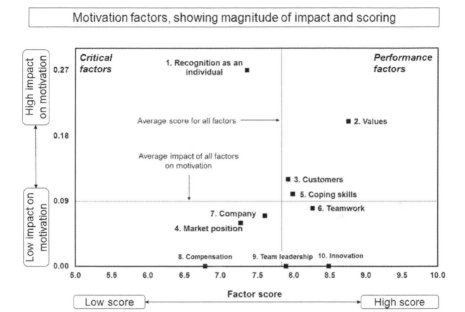

Figure 19. Fourfold table: the effect of factors on motivation and scoring of these factors.

The fourfold table in figure 19 shows the starting points and the general thrust of initiatives to increase motivation. The "critical factors" field refers to factors that are particularly important in terms of their effect on motivation; at the same time, these are factors that employees rate below average, so there is a particularly high potential for development here. In our case study, it is Factor 1, "recognition as individuals," that is the most important; thereafter, we have Factor 7, "Company/reputation," and Factor 4, "Market position."

In working with the critical factors, the "motivational factors" field should not be ignored; in this particular case, we see Factor 2, "Values," Factor 3, "Customer," Factor 5, "Coping skills," and—at the fringe—Factor 6, "Teamwork," in this field. These are the factors that are supported by the majority of all the employees, as is indicated by the above-average positive rating by employees. These factors play a particularly important role in creating solidarity in the company and their influence on motivation is significant. They form—again from the employees' perspective—the key elements of the prevailing culture within this company and one of its main sources of energy. This aspect requires further intensive cultivation.

The factors that do not exert a measurable effect on motivation in this company are Factor 8, "Compensation," Factor 9, "Team leadership," and Factor 10, "Innovation."

This "dashboard" can also be used to record developments over time by tracking the position of the points that represent the individual factors at different times. This would make it possible to determine immediately whether and to what degree there has been movement in the right direction.[97] It is possible to include these developments in the objectives portfolio of senior management.

Nevertheless, we are still some distance away from developing and implementing specific initiatives. One way of arriving at these is to break down the factors as they appear in the company as a whole into the individual business units and from there into their subdivisions.

Figure 20 signposts an initial step toward this process. The motivation, satisfaction, and assessment of the ten factors by the employees are represented by business unit.

At first glance, there are considerable differences between the three business units in all the points represented here. Business unit 1 scores significantly or very significantly higher than the company average for motivation and satisfaction and also for the majority of the ten factors. It is only in the area of "Compensation" and in relation to "Market position" that employee assessment is slightly negative.

---

[97] Creating such time series requires indexing the factors.

Differences in the scoring of factors by business units represented as deviations from the company average (mean value)

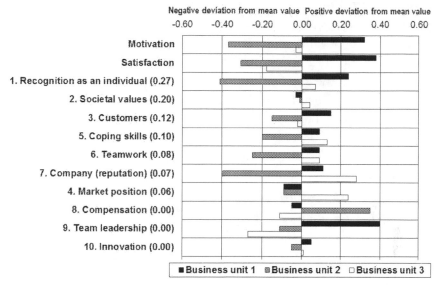

Figure 20. Differences between the business units based on the score for each factor, expressed as deviations from the mean value for the company (n = 425). Bars to the right show positive deviations from the mean value of the company, and bars to the left indicate negative deviations from the average.

The situation in business unit 2 is particularly interesting. Here, motivation and satisfaction can be regarded as critical, since they clearly fall in the negative sector. Two factors are clearly at the center: Factor 1, "Recognition as individuals," and Factor 7, "Company/reputation." The next critical factor is Factor 6, "Teamwork."

Business unit 2 has a history that explains the overall critical attitude with respect to motivation and the majority of the factors at play in motivation. About twelve months before the audit, business unit 2 was acquired and integrated into this company. The result is that this division fell short in the important aspects, as Factors 1, 7, 6, and 3 indicate; the employees of business unit 2 do not feel recognized and valued as individuals, and they do not see the company as a home to be proud of (Factor 7, "Reputation"). This is by no means a question of pay; in terms of "Compensation," the employees of business unit 2 assess their new employer far more positively than their colleagues from the other business units. In other words, the employees of business unit 2 have not yet "settled in" with their new employer—with a corresponding impact on their motivation and, subsequently, their satisfaction. At the same time, the employees of business unit 1 also seem to be somewhat wary of management policy in that they assess their employer's market position (Factor 4) rather negatively. To a certain extent, they are distancing themselves from the company's new focus, this focus being what led to the integration of business unit 2. This further complicates integration of the employees of business unit 2.

Figure 20 indicates that there are problems among the employees of business unit 3, mainly with their immediate team leadership and immediate supervisors. An in-depth analysis by subunit shows that this is a general problem in business unit 3.

The Value Balance in Business audit was designed primarily to analyze a company's corporate culture, with a view to developing this in line with the company philosophy. At this point, it is clear that Value Balance in Business audits are also capable of providing a valuable service in other respects.

1. With mergers, a Value Balance in Business audit provides information on the compatibility of corporate cultures, as well as the new employees' attitude toward and expectations of their new employer. Value Balance in Business audits are useful during the preparation for a merger, as well as for supporting the implementation and possibly also assisting with the post-merger phase.
2. For acquisitions, a Value Balance in Business audit can provide investors with substantial information regarding the current degree of motivation in an organization; it provides guidance as to the extent to which a company already demonstrates a meaning- and performance-centered culture and indications of what a future owner would still need to address in this regard. As a complement to the usual financial and other objective indicators used in determining the value of the company, Value Balance in Business audits provide important additional

information that can substantially reduce the risk associated with investments.

Value Balance in Business audits can be used to take the above analysis by business unit (fig. 20) much further and clarify the starting points for initiatives and their objectives to an even greater extent. This is demonstrated using the example of the seven subunits of business unit 2 (fig. 21).

Figure 21 shows that the employees of business unit 2 form anything but a homogeneous group. The assessment of their situation varies from subunit to subunit. Some of these subunits are particularly noteworthy in this regard—especially subunits 3, 5, and 6.

Subunits 5 and 6 indicate a very negative assessment of the most important motivation factor—Factor 1, "Recognition as individuals." Individual discussions will need to be conducted with the relevant employees to find out why this is the case. In subunit 5, a range of other factors play a role in the comparatively low motivation (and satisfaction) recorded; there is a great divide between these employees and the company, not only around the company's reputation (Factor 7) but also with regard to customer service (Factor 3) and market position (Factor 4). Overall, among the employees of subunit 5, there is deep mistrust of their new employer.

Looking at subunit 3, the audit data indicate severe problems with team leadership (Factor 9), while we can assume an above-average satisfaction in terms of compensation.

This data illustrates that the Value Balance in Business audit provides a differentiated way of looking at the units and subunits, the level of motivation within these, and the assessment of influence factors. In this way, the Value Balance in Business audit identifies each area of the company where the situation needs to be clarified and dealt with in more detail through personal contact with employees (both management and staff). The Value Balance in Business audit does not offer a catch-all solution; it leads to specific initiatives for specific groups of employees.

The more accurate these initiatives are, the more effective and efficient they will be, and the greater are their chances of success.

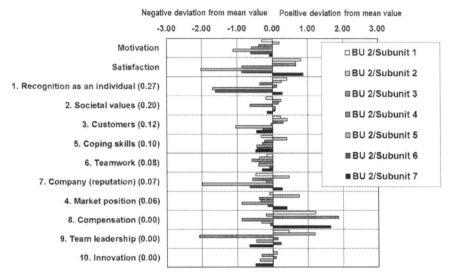

| Business unit 2: Differences in the scoring of factors by business subunits represented as deviations from the company average (mean value) |

Figure 21. Differences between the subunits of business unit 2 with regard to motivation and satisfaction, as well as the assessment of the ten factors (n = 107).

7.5 Grouping of Employees by Disposition

As noted in chapter 6.3.4, the Value Balance in Business audit also allows for Perspective 4, "Employees," to be supplemented with further questions. For example:

- The place work occupies in the life of the employees
- Problem-solving behavior
- Future orientation
- Openness to new ideas, adaptability
- Goal-orientation
- Success-orientation
- Motivation
- Self-conception as a leader or follower

- The need for challenge
- Competitiveness (do employees see themselves as being in competition with others?)
- Continuing education behavior
- Team-orientation
- Collegiality, responsibility for others
- Whether motivation is based on ideals or material factors

Grouping of employees by level of motivation toward the company

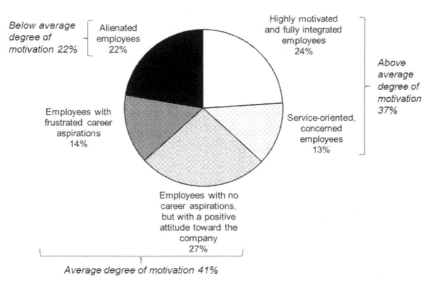

Figure 22. Grouping of employees by disposition (n = 425).

One of many interesting data-reduction and evaluation options for this kind of survey data is cluster analysis. Here, employees with similar response patterns to the type of questions outlined above are grouped together in groups (clusters). The objective of the analysis is to form the most homogeneous groups possible, which should differ as much as possible from the other groups. The motivation and satisfaction of these groups can also be identified. Cluster analyses supplement the results of the factor analysis; in many cases, they are also useful as a countercheck for factor analysis.

For the company presented here, the best solution was found to contain five clusters (fig. 22). These clusters are discussed briefly below:

7.5.1 Explanation of the Five Employee Clusters

a. The highly motivated and fully integrated employee

This cluster represents the 24 percent of employees with the greatest degree of motivation. These employees are characterized by a very optimistic attitude (they see opportunities, not problems); to an extent that is well above average, they see that their own potential for being good for someone or something can be realized through the company; they have great confidence in their coworkers and the company, whose reputation they also view as above average. For them, a good corporate culture is much more important than salary aspects. All in all, they feel very much at home in their company. These are employees for whom the meaning of their work in the company is (almost) a given, and they feel recognized and valued.

b. The service-oriented, concerned employee

These employees demonstrate a high level of motivation, but they nevertheless have a critical attitude toward various aspects of the company. In this particular case, they represent a good eighth of the employees. They are often concerned about the quality of products and services and the company's market position and therefore also about the future of the company—which is relevant to their perception of meaning. This group of *loyal, motivated, and concerned employees* is particularly at risk of burnout. They set high standards for themselves and for the company, and it is invariably difficult to achieve these. As a result, their attitude is correspondingly skeptical. When speaking to these employees, one always gets the impression that there is in them a prevailing sense of abandonment and that at least some of the stress that they are under would be reduced if their superiors were more willing to listen to them.

c. *The employee with no career aspirations but with a positive attitude toward the company*

This group of 27 percent of the employees is distinguished by an average degree of motivation. These employees ascribe a slightly above-average reputation to their company; they do see opportunities to contribute their full potential, and they describe a climate of trust. A disproportionate number of them are part-time female employees, and in most cases, it is not the company that is at the center of their lives but their families. That is also why they do not pursue any career plans. If they did want a career, they might see this as entirely possible, because they assess their employer's promotion of young talent as being above average. They are connected to the company because it offers them good working conditions. In addition, they consider good possibilities for promotion of young talent to be an important sign of appreciation for the individual.

d. *Employees with frustrated career aspirations*

The frustrated career aspirations of this group of employees are not directly evident from the available survey data. Instead, they result from in-depth research within the company. Within the context of this research, the members of this cluster (14 percent of all employees) displayed the following characteristics:

- Average degree of motivation
- Negative assessment of the company's reputation
- Extremely poor assessment of the development of young talent in the company
- Below-average degree of mutual trust
- Very negative assessment regarding the development of their own potential

It may be that these employees display an average degree of motivation, despite having what is sometimes a very skeptical attitude toward the company, because they aspire to a management position, which is associated with a corresponding sense of duty and work ethic. These employees were hit hard by an HR initiative implemented about two years before the Value Balance in Business audit, in which the lowest management level was removed for cost-saving reasons. This meant that these employees lost their former status, which, in terms of recognition and appreciation as individuals, had a profoundly negative effect. Because this change was applied to the lowest and thus broadest of the management levels, it affected a great many employees. The corresponding frustration overshadowed their perception of meaning in the company.

e.   *The alienated employee*

This group represents the 22 percent of employees who have by far the lowest degree of motivation. What is especially striking is the well-below-average awareness these employees have of their contribution to targets, a very negative assessment of the opportunity to contribute their own potential in the company, low mutual trust, and what is clearly a negative attitude toward the company and its reputation. These employees do not feel at home in this company; they are uprooted, and their perception of meaning and recognition in the company is correspondingly low. The result is the very low degree of motivation that has been clearly identified.

This has very little to do with poor work ethics; for two-thirds of the alienated, their work is just as important in their lives as for other employees. The integration of business unit 2 about a year before the implementation of this audit provides an explanation for this alienation to some extent. Business unit 2 has an above-average proportion of alienated employees. In personal discussions, several employees from this business unit pointed out that theirs was the only business unit not represented on the executive board—which they saw as a sign that the company considered them and their business unit to be inferior. This brings us back to the question of recognition and appreciation.

Further cluster analyses show that in the segment with the oldest employees, the proportion of highly motivated, fully integrated employees is by far the highest, which is an indication of long-term loyalty.

7.5.2   Employee Clusters and Their Share in Various Business Areas

Composition of managers/employees, business units, and function groups by clusters

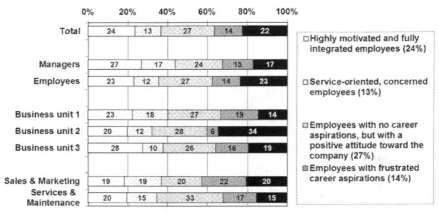

Figure 23. Employee clusters by business units, and function groups (n = 425).

The "Total" row at the top of figure 23 shows the overall grouping of employees into clusters (fig. 22). There are a few points that are of particular note:

- As explained previously, business unit 2 is the result of an acquisition that took place well over a year before this audit was conducted. This business unit has not yet integrated successfully. It is therefore not surprising that, among the employees of business unit 2, the number of alienated employees is disproportionately large and comprises more than 34 percent of all employees.
- Among the managers, 17 percent belong to the group of "alienated employees." In terms of the multiplier effect that managers have, this poses a problem.
- In the Sales and Marketing Department, four out of ten employees either belong to the group of alienated employees or to the group of employees with frustrated career aspirations—which is more than the average for the entire company. This is especially problematic due to their contact with customers; this division shapes the

image of the company to a large degree (employee branding is a factor here). The possible consequences for sales/revenue, relationship maintenance with the customers, or the impact on customer loyalty are clear. Nevertheless, it should be noted that two-thirds of alienated employees have a high work ethic and that the employees' frustration with disappointed career aspirations is also self-inflicted. In the interest of internal values and a climate of trust, the company would do well to work together with the relevant employees to find solutions to this problem.

–   At 19 percent, the group of service-oriented, concerned employees represents a higher than average proportion in the Sales and Marketing Department. The company should see this as a serious warning sign; it is possible that the concerns expressed by these employees are the result of feedback from customers. Then again, one should also not overlook the fact that employees with customer contact sometimes overestimate the performance of competitors and underestimate the benefits of their own company. While it is essential for management to consult with employees who have contact with customers, it is equally vital to consult independent sources when gathering information on customers and products.

7.6   Developing a Portfolio of Initiatives and Tracking Current and Target Scores

The above example shows some facets of interpreting the data gathered by the employee survey. Careful analysis of the data reveals:

1.   In which divisions of the company it would be of benefit (to both the employees and the company) to undertake initiatives in order to increase motivation
2.   In which direction these initiatives should lead

A considerable component of the data analysis and the resulting proposals for initiatives is based on assessment aspects that are surveyed in the Value Balance in Business audit and are included in the factor analysis (see table 11). These can be seen as an equivalent to the Key

Performance Indicators (KPIs) of the Balanced Scorecard. Because they are mainly in quantified form—whether in percentages or evaluations or average values—the current and target scores can be included in a tracking table of initiatives (see table 12).

The current data has been entered in the example tracking table for initiatives shown below. However, when preparing tracking tables for initiatives, one must not forget the points that could not be surveyed and for which there is no quantitative data available. In this survey, therefore, the "mission" and "vision" aspects are absent, because this company did not have any at the time the Value Balance in Business audit was conducted. From the viewpoint of a meaning- and performance-centered corporate culture, development of these aspects is essential and must therefore be the first item to be entered in the portfolio of initiatives.

The inclusion of the current data in table 12 represents the last step in a company audit. The definition of the target data and the associated initiatives is the next task for those who lead and implement the development of the corporate culture and the organizational and staff development.

It is of crucial importance to the success of these initiatives that they are not decided upon and implemented over the heads of the employees involved but in cooperation with them. This approach is consistent with the fundamental postulate of meaning and recognition outlined in the Value Balance in Business, as applied in a meaning- and performance-centered corporate culture.

Another audit is appropriate after the implementation phase in order to compare the new current scores with the target after carrying out the proposed initiatives. In this way, the success of the initiatives can be evaluated, and any divergence between the new current and target scores can be analyzed.

The Value Balance in Business thus provides a tool that allows for the systematic capture and management of important elements that are relevant to employee motivation and the resulting performance of the company (see fig. 24).

Initiatives	Assessment perspectives Key Performance Indicators (KPIs)	Current	Target	Delta	Company perspectives
Development of the mission	KPI: "Mission elicits enthusiasm" (in percentages)	No data			2: Mission, vision, values
Development of the vision	KPI: "Vision elicits enthusiasm" (in percentages)	No data			
Recognition as individuals (0.27)	KPI: Respecting employees as individuals	7.0			1: Leadership
Company/reputation (0.07)	KPI: Company as industry leader	7.4			5: Market position
Market position (0.06)	KPI: Assessment of the reputation of the products in the home market	6.8			5: Market position
Business unit 2: Integration					1: Leadership 3: Customers
In general	**Factor 6: Teamwork** KPI: Team success over personal success	7.0			4: Employees 5: Market position 6: Reputation
	Factor 5: Coping skills KPI: Ability to tolerate uncertainty	7.6			
	Motivation	7.7			
Integration of subunit 5	**Factor 1: Recognition as individuals** KPI: Respect for employees	6.6			
	Factor 3: Customers (mean value of all KPIs) KPI: Degree to which customers and their needs are important to employees KPI: Assessment of the company's competitiveness in the industry	6.3			
	Factor 7: Reputation (mean value of all KPIs) KPI: Company's future prospects KPI: Mission elicits enthusiasm KPI: Company as industry leader KPI: Proud of the company	5.6			

Initiatives	Assessment perspectives Key Performance Indicators (KPIs)	Current	Target	Delta	Company perspectives
	Factor 4: Market position (mean value) KPI: Assessment of the reputation of the products in the home market *Motivation*	5.1 7.2			
Integration of subunit 6	**Factor 1: Recognition as individuals** KPI: Respect for employees *Motivation*	5.4 7.7			
Integration of subunit 3	**Factor 9: Team leadership** (mean value of all KPIs) KPI: Supervisors seek the opinions of employees KPI: Supervisors support employees, especially in difficult situations KPI: Loyalty toward employees KPI: Employees feel acknowledged as individuals *Motivation*	5.8 7.9			
Business unit 3: Immediate supervisors	KPI: Team leadership *Motivation*	8.0 5.3			
Sales and Marketing	Reduction of proportion of "Alienated employees" (%) Reduction of proportion of "Frustrated employees" (%) Reduction of proportion of "Concerned employees" (%) *Motivation*	20.0 22.0 19.0 8.5			1: Leadership
Managers	Reduction of proportion of "Alienated employees" (%) *Motivation*	20.0 *8.5*			1: Leadership
Overall degree of motivation	***Overall motivation in the company***	*8.3*			**1: Leadership**

Table 12. The Value Balance in Business audit tracking table for initiatives.

The monitoring process based on the *Value Balance in Business*

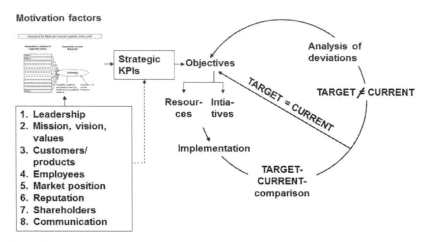

Figure 24. Model of the monitoring process based on the Value Balance in Business audit.

7.7 Value Balance in Business and Balanced Scorecard

As noted previously, the Value Balance in Business borrows certain concepts from the Balanced Scorecard (BSC). However, these two worlds are completely independent from each other in that each can function as a stand-alone tool.

Nevertheless, as the company's powerhouse or source of energy, the Value Balance in Business is situated upstream of the BSC and other approaches to business strategy. There are also certain aspects in the Value Balance in Business and the BSC that complement each other and that might be of interest for both approaches:

- *Customer satisfaction:* If, according to BSC indicators, this aspect is in decline, it is worth looking into the corresponding section of the Value Balance in Business: How do employees rate customer satisfaction, products and services (value for money, quality), and the quality of their contact with customers?

Employees often express criticism of products and services and the quality of customer contact even before dissatisfaction among customers becomes widespread. An assessment of customer satisfaction using the Value Balance in Business can serve as an early indicator of the state of affairs in this regard. In addition, a negative evaluation of products and services and/or customer contact by employees has negative consequences for employee motivation and commitment.

- *Learning and growth perspective of the BSC/Value Balance in Business Perspective 4, "Employees":* Here there are distinct overlaps with some BSC items, such as "Participation in decision making," "Recognition of performance," "Support from the personnel department," and in particular "General satisfaction." These variables also appear in the Value Balance in Business in some or other form.

- *"Employee loyalty" (BSC) and "Employee commitment" in the Value Balance in Business:* These two indicators may be in sync. However, if, according to the BSC, employee loyalty remains high, meaning if there is little staff turnover, while at the same time the Value Balance in Business indicates that employee commitment is decreasing, this could be an indication that employees are experiencing stress.

- The BSC places particular emphasis on *improvement indicators.* In this regard, its relationship with the Value Balance in Business is also complementary: the Value Balance in Business provides a summary, as evaluated by the employees, of how proposals for innovation are handled in the company, while the BSC records the number of specific submissions. It may, for example, be interesting to see whether, according to the Value Balance in Business, feedback from supervisors regarding suggestions improves from the perspective of the employees and how this trend correlates with the number of specific proposals for innovation received according to the BSC.

"Culture eats strategy!" The Value Balance in Business is upstream of the Balanced Scorecard; in general, a company's culture changes much more slowly than its strategy. What this means is that a sound corporate culture supports the development and implementation of strategies in a company by creating a favorable context, as well as by providing the energy needed for successful implementation within the company. However, corporate culture cannot simply be created in the short term based on the strategy and immediately applied in its service. Corporate culture—and the Value Balance in Business—cannot be subordinate to corporate strategy. Different periods in a particular corporate culture generally last longer than cycles in corporate strategy, and because of this difference in the lifespan or duration of validity of these two aspects, they can only very rarely be brought into line.

7.8 The Value Balance in Business Audit Process

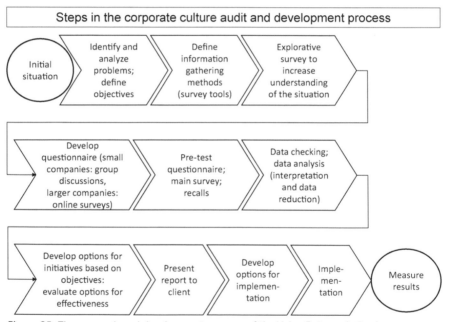

Figure 25. The research and development process of the Value Balance in Business.

Because it is such an important process, a Value Balance in Business audit is usually commissioned by the top executive bodies (by the supervisory or executive board and/or the CEO/senior executive officers), provided that they are also included in the survey. Data collection normally takes place in the form of a conventional research process. For a medium-sized company, about twelve weeks should be allocated for this.

7.9 Developing and Maintaining the Corporate Culture

7.9.1 Allocation of Responsibilities and Approach to the Development of Corporate Culture

The assessment or audit process that we have just outlined can be implemented as it stands if the cornerstones of corporate culture are already present in the company—especially the mission, vision, and values. If these are not yet in place, they will first need to be developed. There are several methods to achieve this, and the responsibilities for each topic should be allocated specifically (see table 13).

The development of the mission and vision (and subsequent maintenance of these) falls into the area of responsibility of the top executive bodies. Through the mission, they establish the guiding star of the company's activities, and through the vision, they define the company's challenging and specific long-term development goals.

The third core element of the spirit of the company, which is another way to view corporate culture, is the company's values. This is the most tangible aspect of corporate culture; even those who are entirely unaware of the company's mission and vision inevitably come into contact with the company's values. In terms of external values (utility values and relationship values), it is highly advisable for companies to listen to their customers as well as their employees. The key idea here is a "solution-free analysis of customer problems."

Topic	Initiator/source	Feedback
Mission	Defined and formulated by the top executive bodies.	Consultative dialogue with employees: evaluating its attractiveness (does the mission excite the employees, ignite a spark in them?)

Topic	Initiator/source	Feedback
Vision	Defined and formulated by the top executive bodies.	Consultative dialogue with employees: evaluating its attractiveness (does the vision inspire employees?)
Values	Internal values: Survey of current and target among all employees. External values: Survey of current and target among employees and customers. Possibly additionally target values for management from a strategic perspective.	Selection and prioritization of values: employees at all levels are involved; customers are involved for utility and relationship values.

Table 13. Allocation of responsibilities in developing a corporate culture in a large SME.

A clear distinction must be made between the company's current and target values, between what the situation currently is and what the situation is desired to be in the future. If senior management presents the desired situation as the current reality, this is likely to provoke dangerous cynicism among employees. This does not mean that no target values can be introduced into the process; it will, however, require careful implementation.

To check whether the mission and vision are likely to ignite a spark that will transmit enthusiasm to all employees, it is important that a meaningful dialogue be conducted with the employees. To gain feedback on the company's values, our recommendation is to proceed using a consultation process and to let all the employees participate, either directly or indirectly (via a representative or a sample). There are a variety of ways to approach this, from one-on-one interviews to large group events.[98]

---

[98] See in particular Matthias zur Bonsen, *Lebendigkeit im Unternehmen Freisetzen und Nutzen* [Leading with life: releasing and using vitality in companies]. 1st edition.

The Value Balance in Business checklist for defining the main components that lie at the core of a meaning- and performance-centered corporate culture includes the following items (see chapter 4 for a detailed description of each item):

1. The *mission* (anchoring the company in a higher value or ideal, in line with Peter Drucker)
2. The *vision* as the concise embodiment of a specific but ambitious development goal for the company (the mountain we want to climb together)
3. *Internal values* with a focus on mutual recognition and respect for intentions and motives
4. *Utility values of the products/services* for the customers (resolving customer issues in accordance with the customer's intentions/ motives)
5. *Relationship values* in customer contact (respect, recognition)
6. *Reliability as an employer* (see chapter 4.6.2)
7. *Responsible use of environmental resources* (see chapter 4.6.2)
8. Optional: The status of shareholders, dealing with suppliers, working with communities/authorities/institutions, employee codes of conduct, and the like (chapter 4.6.2)

Items 1 through 7 are essential for defining the core components of a meaning- and performance-centered corporate culture. The optional items may also apply, depending on the company's specific situation.

In addressing these points, it could prove very helpful to form a team who could do the groundwork for management and formulate proposals for mission, vision, and values as described above. The company might already have a culture team or corporate climate group. Ideally, this team would be composed of employees from all hierarchical levels, functional areas, and branches of business, each with one vote. Preparation of the individual topics can be delegated to subgroups if required.

These teams usually grasp the relevant points quite well. A group that constitutes a representative cross section of the company also promotes

Wiesbaden: Gabler, 2009.

acceptance among employees; here, the aspect of recognition and participation plays an important role: "One of us was also there and was able to voice our concerns."

> The more prudently a development process is carried out, the more widely it is supported; the more employees at all levels are involved directly, the more sustainable and performance enhancing the company's culture will be.

7.9.2 Mission, Vision, and Values—Greater Visibility Means Greater Effectiveness

Once the heart or the core of a corporate culture—its mission, vision, and values—has been determined, we come to yet another crucial point: a culture can only be effective if the individuals concerned understand exactly what this will mean for them in their day-to-day work.

This requires that the entire management team be completely familiar with the topics covered in the checklist in chapter 7.9.1 and that they be aware of what these topics mean in detail for their own management levels. Once this understanding is in place, managers will need to hold a team meeting together with their staff—and whenever possible, with the presence of senior management—to determine the contribution that their team can make to the mission, the objectives for the team arising from the vision, and how the internal and external values—utility values and relationship values—can be put into practice, as well as the contribution they can make to this.

The focus is on applying the company's mission, vision, and values to the team's specific situation. At the same time, this is an important aspect of participation: in this way, these three perspectives of the company also become the perspectives of the employees. In carrying out this process, it is useful to accurately determine initiatives, deadlines, and responsibilities and to track progress in these.

The following shows some specific example questions that could be used to develop the checklist for use by individual teams or groups:

- How is the work we do in our team related to the customer's utility and relationship values? Where are we directly involved? What does this mean for us? *Who* among us is involved? *What* do we need to do specifically? *How* should this be done?
- If we are not in direct contact with customers, how can we help ensure that customers have an optimal experience? *How* can we, through our work, best support our colleagues who are directly in contact with customers? *What* does this specifically mean for us?
- What should mutual respect and mutual recognition look like in our team? How can we—and do we want to—put this into practice? How do we interact with each other when we come from different cultural backgrounds? Are we able to see these differences as enriching and use them productively?
- What resources are needed by our team in order to live these values? Does this require training or coaching? Do we need tools, or do we just need feedback, a continuous exchange with our internal and/or external customers?

Ideally, it is not just teams as a whole who answer these questions; instead, each team member can consider his or her contribution and submit suggestions to the team. The team members can then discuss the questions, give feedback, and come to an agreement on each one, especially in relation to the internal values.

Another important point is a *binding agreement* on times and occasions when the core elements of corporate culture will be addressed on an ongoing basis. Defining the values, mission, and vision once and launching these concepts at a company event is not enough—it is merely the kickoff for the company's cultural development. It is important that they are touched upon on a regular basis. Ideally, they should be encountered every day in order that they remain visible at all times, or even better, that they become embodied in all employees at all levels. This is best done by defining specific occasions when this will take place. There are countless opportunities for reiterating the core elements of the company's culture and for institutionalizing a discourse on values—and they can be applied in a cumulative way. Here are just a few ideas on how this can be achieved:

- Daily—for example, during progress report meetings, using visual media in specific areas in the company, by referencing them in communications (especially in relation to management decisions)
- The weekly team meeting
- Regular personal reporting between the employee and his or her immediate supervisor
- During the employee assessment
- In agreements with employees about the objectives for the coming year
- In "refresher courses" for all employees every year or two
- In induction courses with new employees
- In internal media (e.g., on an intranet platform)
- In CEO road shows
- In management meetings and seminars
- At corporate events, anniversaries, parties
- In meetings held by management and governing bodies; here, it is recommended to not merely address the topic from time to time but to consistently check each decision for its compatibility with the company's mission, vision, and values[99]

The questions asked on such occasions always point in the same direction. Where have we put our mission, vision, and values into practice? Where have we done this well, and where we have failed to do so? How can we avoid this next time? Do we need to take any special action here? Where and how can we improve? When faced with disputes or conflicts, do we always refer to these three guiding principles, especially to the mission as

---

[99] This may seem laborious, but it could somewhat shorten and facilitate discussions. Discussions would be more focused; conflicts of interest, departmental egotism, or even power struggles would become transparent much more rapidly; the heart of the matter would be laid bare more quickly; discussions would begin with the fundamentals less often or peter out into these less often than if these had never been agreed upon; not to mention the effect of this kind of decision making in particular on lower and middle management and staff.

our ultimate guide? Do we always check if the answers to our problems can be found in these?

In institutionalizing a corporate culture, the mission, vision, and values must also be taken into consideration in the *company procedures,* especially in *human resources development.* Important steps can be taken at the *recruitment* stage; employment interviews and assessments are a good opportunity to garner substantial information regarding a future employee's affinity for the company culture, and in employment contracts, the mission and values form part of the components that must be subscribed to specifically.

A clear image of the company right from the first point of contact is a strong source of persuasion and motivation for future employees. A coherent picture of a good corporate culture includes how present and future employees and their families are treated as well as how the company deals with former employees—whether they are included at corporate events, for example—and in particular, whether the dignity of those involved in dismissals is respected.

Only those who adhere to the mission, vision, and values themselves have the right to demand the same of others. In this respect, supervisors have a particular function and responsibility as *role models.* Firstly, they are called upon to consistently practice and exemplify the mission, vision, and values and then to consistently demand the same of their staff. Under these conditions, the employee should also have the right to demand that their supervisors practice these values.

In the ongoing development and maintenance of corporate culture, it is also necessary to provide opportunities to ask basic questions about the mission, vision, and values. *Which of these are still relevant? How can they be adapted to new circumstances?* It is important that the *spirit* of a company's mission, vision, and values should remain valid for as long as possible, but their interpretation and their practical implementation should be adapted to the ever-changing conditions. It is management's responsibility to ensure this process.

7.9.3 Personal Character and Professional Expertise

A sustainable, performance-enhancing corporate culture is based on values. If these are put into practice consistently at all levels, the culture will survive. Ultimately, whether somebody adheres to it or not is a question of character, and while character is one thing, professional expertise is another. The question is, which carries more weight?

Time and again, we see how, with somebody who has highly developed professional expertise, companies look the other way when this person does not demonstrate their values (and yet, almost as often, they admit that they had waited too long and intervened too late).

People who violate the values of a company and are not penalized for it provoke uncertainty, and this rubs off on the employees. More than that, when values are put into practice, work becomes easier for managers and employees alike. Values have this facilitating effect due to their function of setting the direction and guidelines for decision making; they guide employees' actions toward common goals and provide support in the decision-making process. They thus create conditions under which the members of a company can focus on their core functions. They unburden managers in their operational activities and help to avoid conflicts—or to find sustainable solutions for conflicts. Not living the values robs the company of valuable strength. When trust is lacking, more monitoring is needed; when issuing directives, one must always get back to basics. Conflicts[100] and power struggles arise in teams and between leaders and employees ... the list goes on.

---

[100] These could have dramatic repercussions. One US study claims that destructive, unsocial behavior can lead to a significant breakdown in the performance of those on the receiving end of such behavior from their colleagues. According to a survey among thousands of executives and employees in the United States, 48 percent of those affected reduced their commitment to their work, 47 percent reduced their working hours, 38 percent spoke of a decline in the quality of their work, 66 percent said their performance had declined, 80 percent lost time during processing of corresponding incidents, 63 percent lost time in an effort to avoid the aggressor, 78 percent said their loyalty to the company have suffered. See Porath and Pearson, "How Toxic Colleagues Corrode Performance."

Against this backdrop, Helmut Maucher, honorary president of Nestlé, had this motto: "Look more in their eyes than in their files. If I am faced with somebody who only improves him- or herself narcissistically—no, there is nothing I can do with such a person."[101] Somebody who does not contribute their best professionally can in many cases be transferred to a position in the company where he or she can apply their skills adequately and be of service; somebody who for reasons of character does not adhere to the values of their company must, on the other hand, expect quick and clear consequences.

---

[101] Helmut Maucher, interview in *Persönlich* (December 2001), 12.

8. What the Value Balance in Business Offers—A Cultural Balance Sheet

There is no difference between the
corporate life, my personal life or ordinary
life, because ethics is needed everywhere.
—Nicolas Hayek, former chairman and delegate
of the board of directors, Swatch Group

8.1 The Value Balance in Business: A Signpost to Coevolution and Fertile Ground Where Companies Can Create Shared Value

Meaning is the missing link between individual and company, the cement that holds the structure together. Meaning makes it possible to explain collective action at the corporate level without detracting from the employee's individuality and guiding principles. This is because meaning implies freedom of choice for the individual while remaining mindful of the responsibility toward a collective greater whole. When we talk about meaning, we cannot speak of "freedom from" something but only of the "freedom to practice responsibility" (toward a meaningful greater whole).

In a fundamental sense, individuals find the meaning of their actions in their relationship to the collective, such as their relationship to the company as a whole as a provider of services to customers, shareholders, and society (see fig. 9 and 10). The company acquires its right to exist from being of service to individuals—in other words, customers, employees, members of the community, and its shareholders. It gives equal importance to the individual and the collective, and neither nor the other is considered to be merely there for the benefit of the other.

This relationship is one of reciprocal service, which in turn leads us to the idea of coevolution being the antithesis of the maximization of self-interest.

The original idea behind this concept derives from philosophical anthropology, with its image of an individual who is open toward the world. Based on this image, Viktor Frankl painted his picture of a human being who has the freedom to practice responsibility. Another of Frankl's ideas that is crucial to our approach is that meaning provides both motivation and orientation for our actions and that meaning is found through taking action.

The meaning-centered philosophy represented here opens up a new approach to corporate culture, which is built upon two pillars:

1. *Meaning and recognition* as the primary, existential sources of employee *motivation* and commitment
2. *The company's performance* for the benefit of customers and society as the reason for its existence—as its meaning

As an approach toward a meaning- and performance-centered corporate culture, the Value Balance in Business connects these two pillars through *mission, vision, and values.* They are the employees' source of meaning/recognition and motivation through the resulting benefits for customers and society, and they also constitute the source of the company's right to exist, as well as the basis of its *economic* function and success (see fig. 26). Meaning, mission, and vision create a parallel, mutually reinforcing relationship between employee motivation and the economic and social requirements on the company's performance.

The freedom to practice responsibility is associated with the freedom people have to start their own business or to choose an employer with a specific mission, vision, and values. This choice goes hand in hand with personal acceptance of (co)responsibility for these three elements and for the company in the service of coevolution and the sustainable promotion of life.[102]

---

[102] In this context, one could also speak of "pragmatic ethics." It does not present an obstacle to the company's success but rather a necessary—albeit insufficient—condition

In its identification of these key concepts and the way that they interact, this book presents a conceptual tool for a meaning- and performance-centered corporate culture and an analytical instrument with which to perform corporate culture audits. While this tool clearly does not encompass all the facets of a corporate culture, the Value Balance in Business does contain the constitutive elements, and it significantly reduces the complexity of corporate cultures. At the same time, it offers substantial information about their constitution and how to use this to systematically develop them further toward employee performance and motivation, as well as coevolution and the sustainable promotion of life. In this sense, it is also the paradigm within which the concept of shared value can reach its full potential.

> *Value Balance in Business:* Mission, vision and values as employees' sources of meaning and motivation, and as company's source of performance and success

Figure 26. The core elements of the Value Balance in Business corporate culture concept and audit.

for the company's continued success.

8.2   The Economic Benefits and Potential Risks of a Meaning- and Performance-Centered Corporate Culture

8.2.1   Benefits

The main impact of a meaning- and performance-centered corporate culture lies in the mobilization of people's spiritual capital. This in turn has many positive effects on different aspects of the performance and viability of companies and other institutions, including:

- The will to perform (employees' spiritual ability to perform and disposition toward personal growth)
- Employees' willingness to assume responsibility, commitment to the company's objectives, loyalty toward the company (as long as the company remains true to its mission, vision, and values)
- Disposition for effectively creating shared value
- An exchange of experience/knowledge; balanced distribution and widespread accumulation of knowledge through open communication
- The willingness to cooperate based on common binding objectives
- Constructive conflict-management skills instead of playing power games; letting the better idea prevail for customers and society
- Customer loyalty through a primacy of performance in favor of the customers (utility and relationship values)
- A willingness to change/propensity to innovate, (i.e., the willingness to adapt internally, to include strategy, products, processes, structures) and externally (to include customer needs, competitive situation, economic development in the industry and the national economy)
- The ability to differentiate products and services in the market; decreasing substitutability, greater autonomy in pricing
- Creativity and ingenuity

- A climate that promotes health (salutogenesis as per Aaron Antonovsky)[103] through mutual recognition and freedom to decide on/structure one's own work (meaning)
- High level of employee commitment to the company (long-term commitment as an aspect of recruitment)
- Reduced absenteeism in the company as a factor of individual employees' productivity
- Efficient and effective structures and processes—the 6-f-business: fit, fast, flexible, focused, friendly, fulfilling to work for
- Social reputation and the associated access to important material and immaterial resources
- A reduction in expenses related to management, human resources, marketing
- A high capacity for external adaptation and internal integration within the company, drawing on many early warning indicators (employee motivation/climate, products, customers, reputation)
- Financial performance, adaptability, and survivability
- Strengthening of the company's environment as a result of coevolution: customers, shareholders, society, and the natural environment create a positive context for continued development of the company

Many of these positive effects are mutually reinforcing and self-perpetuating. However, the negative effects of a dysfunctional corporate culture are equally enduring.

There are various economic effects of a healthy corporate culture that can be quantified well using quantitative models. Gallup indicates that a higher degree of employee loyalty toward the company reduces staff turnover and absenteeism to such a degree that, in Germany, it results in cost savings of nearly €1 million for a company with five hundred employees and €4 million for a company with two thousand employees.[104]

---

[103] Aaron Antonovsky, *Unraveling The Mystery of Health—How People Manage Stress and Stay Well* (San Francisco: Jossey-Bass Publishers, 1987).
[104] Gallup, Engagement Index Germany 2008, January 14, 2009, Potsdam.

Heskett[105] also presents quantitative models that point to the comparative advantages of companies with a healthy corporate culture in terms of:

- Cost savings through a reduction in employee recruitment costs (in that existing employees recruit new employees, and employees tend to remain with these companies longer)
- Employee productivity
- Acquiring and retaining customers.

Because of the diverse situations in different companies, no specific figures will be disclosed here. Suffice it to say that the comparative advantages of a healthy culture can be quite substantial. (However, in our opinion it is not this but rather mankind's distinction as a being endowed with spirituality that forms the definitive reason for nurturing a meaning- and performance-centered corporate culture.)

8.2.2 Potential Risks

A number of renowned authors have rightly pointed out the risks of an (initially) healthy corporate culture. It is at the moment of greatest success that these risks present the biggest threat. This threat is particularly insidious when the impression of success causes a pervasive belief that we now know "what makes the customer tick" and that nothing could go wrong anymore. Although the customer still remains the focus of the company when this is the case ("we are very customer oriented"), the company now takes its focus off the customer and turns it inward ("we now know once and for all what our customers want"). The result is that the company loses its capacity for self-transcendence and thus its adaptability—it loses its capacity for innovation.

Collins distinguishes five stages for this kind of downfall:[106]

---

[105] James Heskett, *The Culture Cycle: How to Shape the Unseen Force That Transforms Performance* (New Jersey: FT Press, 2012), 97ff.
[106] Collins, *How the Mighty Fall and Why Some Companies Never Give In*, 20.

1. Hubris born of success
2. Undisciplined pursuit of more
3. Denial of risk and peril
4. Grasping for salvation
5. Capitulation to irrelevance and death

Undisciplined pursuit of more can be seen in the exploitation of economies of scale at the expense of innovation as well as in growth that occurs inorganically and too fast.

Heskett points out another important aspect: ineffective measurement:[107] "As organizations approach their peak performance levels, managers typically wait for declines in financial performance before taking action to reverse the trend. ... But there is substantial evidence that the time these measures peak, it may already be too late. ... Warnings of impending problems begin when employee engagement, 'ownership,' and loyalty start to fail"—or when uncertainty about the general validity of the mission, vision, and values spreads among employees; when they start to signal dissatisfaction with the products and services, customer relationships, or the innovation and adaptability of the company; when they express the feeling that their company's market position is deteriorating; or when their trust in senior management starts waning. In its function as an early warning system, the Value Balance in Business is a reliable tool for detecting these and other relevant elements and their changes over time.

An important measure that can help companies avoid succumbing to arrogance or even hubris is to consistently focus on a mission in the form of an ideal and to consistently track the company's status in relation to this in a self-critical way. An ideal is never reachable; you can approach it step by step, but it never allows you to rest on your laurels. Likewise, an inspiring vision is an important source of healthy ambition.

---

[107] Heskett, *The Culture Cycle*, 86.

8.3 The Value Balance in Business and Its Contribution to a More Efficient and Effective Economy

The belief that the pursuit of self-interest is people's ultimate motive is a reductionist concept, because it takes into account only our instincts and psyche and excludes mankind's spiritual and cultural dimension (fig. 6). Therefore the theory of self-serving motivation can be seen as a form of natural determinism. As beings that live for nothing but self-interest, we thus find ourselves in the world of Darwinian natural selection, of natural evolution on the basis of survival of the fittest. The short-term view by which *Homo economicus* operates is a necessary reaction to the "law of the jungle".

The meaning- and performance-centered approach of coevolution is in direct contrast to this motivation theory in that we humans have, through our participation in the spiritual and cultural world, emancipated ourselves from the natural environment. This is how we achieve freedom and, in the future, take on even more responsibility toward this environment.

In the corporate world, coevolution means differentiation and innovation that is in harmony with people, society, and nature. It stands for togetherness—albeit precarious. It is not about always and automatically seeing ourselves as adversaries in the quest for personal gain. Survival of the fittest in the Darwinian sense means aggressively accumulating as many resources for yourself as possible at the expense of others—this is the world of *Homo economicus*. Survival of the fittest in the sense of coevolution and a meaning- and performance-centered motivation theory means fitting into the greater whole to the greatest possible degree in which the best possible contribution is made to finding a solution for the shared problems experienced by the greater whole. As a result of this, everyone becomes stronger, which in turn is to the advantage of the original provider of services.

Some of the characteristics and consequences of these two approaches—the primacy of profit maximization and that of a focus on coevolution and meaning and performance—are compared in a simplified way in table 14, which shows the two extremes of these paradigms. The utilitarian model is characterized by:

- The mimicking of seemingly lucrative businesses/business models/business areas in order to maximize short-term profits while minimizing risk (the herd instinct, creating economic bubbles in the process)
- Costly Darwinian crowding out and battles for market share due to the high substitutability of products as a result of this imitation
- Fast withdrawal from business activities when times are uncertain in order to minimize cost and risk (the herd instinct, the bubbles burst)

The result is an unnecessarily high variance between a fast, short-term buildup in periods of growth (i.e., unproductive overshooting) and a fast, short-term reduction of employees, physical capital, and customer relations and customer services in the face of imminent crises (i.e., unproductive undershooting). This phenomenon of unproductive over- and undershooting is a hindrance to the continuous, organic accumulation of capital and the steady productivity gains that result from this. Like Sisyphus, *Homo economicus* is forever taking two steps forward and (at least) one step back between ups and downs because of this short-term approach. This is far more strenuous and uneconomical than a less oscillating but prudent, steady advance guided by coevolution and the company's mission, vision, and values.

In the utilitarian paradigm, self-interested competition is often presented as the approach that generates the highest possible customer utility. As already mentioned, this competition may, however, have outcomes that provide anything but the highest customer utility. Competitors may fight each other directly and weaken each other at the expense of customers and customer utility, or oligopolies or monopolies may result. When competitors in the utilitarian Darwinian struggle for existence become war-weary; they try to gain the upper hand through collusions and cartels, which usually do nothing to promote customer utility. By contrast, coevolution's meaning- and performance-centered approach places optimal performance for customers and society at the center of its considerations; they are the company's sources of strength and motivation.

The paradigm of maximization of self-interest	The paradigm of coevolution
• Driver: self-interest, appropriation of the world, propelled by natural drives and urges/giving free reign to these	• Driver: meaning, freedom and responsibility, helping to shape the world, self-realization/self-creation
• Unrelenting laws of nature: limited time horizon (short-term approach)	• Culture: time horizon is not necessarily limited (long-term approach is "conceivable")
• Darwinian natural evolution: survival of the fittest = the law of the strongest	• Coevolution: survival of the fittest = the law of the most willing and able to adapt and cooperate
• Crowding out competitors in order to strengthen one's own position	• Innovate to optimize performance in favor of the greater whole and customers
• Conflict: the battle for resources, all with the same weapons: quantity, price, me too/more of the same, aggressiveness	• Adaptation: differentiation, creativity, competition for better customer solutions
• Mimicking in lucrative areas: accumulation of risks (bubbles)	• Differentiation: reduction of risks
• Focus: competitors (fought in various ways, not just through products and services)	• Focus: customers, society (mission)
• Distant from customers due to the focus on the competitors: high risk of bad investments in innovations, low degree of customer loyalty, expensive push marketing	• Close to customers due to the focus on products and services for the customers: reduced risk of bad investments in innovations, high degree of customer loyalty, economical pull marketing
• Extrinsic motivation and the cost of supervision make the labor force more expensive and decrease productivity	• Intrinsic motivation and trust make the labor force more economical and increase productivity

The paradigm of maximization of self-interest	The paradigm of coevolution
• Market coverage: high, short-term investments, investments in material assets, little investment in human resources	• Continuous adjustment and rededication; investment in people as the bearers of core competencies and agents of lasting change
• Faster, intermittent capacity building	• Organic, steady development
In crises: • People's spiritual abilities are ignored: employee productivity is underestimated • Labor costs are overestimated, savings through layoffs are overestimated • Many unnecessary layoffs in the short term • Intangible damages such as loss of customer satisfaction/ loyalty, innovation and creativity not realized	In crises: • People are the strongest link: much is *invested* in people; an attempt is made to hold on to employees as the bearers of core competencies for as long as possible • Because people are relatively inexpensive, they are not high on the list of savings • Because people are productive, there are relatively fewer layoffs necessary in order to achieve productivity goals • Minor reduction in products and customer services
• Rapid, intermittent reduction in capacity with a particular focus on employees • Unnecessary destruction of expertise, and of trust and loyalty of employees	• Organic cutbacks in capacity, employees less strongly affected • Preservation of expertise, and of trust and loyalty of employees
• Stark, intermittent increase and decrease in investments and human resources: high variance	• Steadier increase and decrease in investment and human resources: low variance

The paradigm of maximization of self-interest	The paradigm of coevolution
• High variance: less continuous capital accumulation, lower productivity gains	• Low variance: capital stock including employee expertise is accumulated continuously, increased growth in productivity
• Competition: creative destruction	• Competition: creative discovery process
• Economy as an end in itself → no reward from the "invisible hand"	• Economy in an exchange of performance with society → access to economically highly significant resources

Table 14. Facets of profit maximization and a meaning- and performance-centered approach.

It is the employees in particular who are affected by the variance between ups and downs outlined above. Inefficient use of their potential in the utilitarian paradigm makes their labor appear more expensive than it is in reality—their productivity is underestimated (fig. 6) and their costs overestimated accordingly.

With a view to cost-saving goals, layoffs are consequently performed too hastily and to a greater extent than is justified by the employees' actual productivity. Human labor is therefore underestimated in its importance compared to other factors of production and not utilized to a great enough extent—this especially affects women and both younger and older people, with their own specific skills. There is significant potential lying fallow, particularly in the form of unemployment, to the detriment of the people concerned as well as society and the corporate world.

Companies are at an advantage in terms of their performance and profitability if they allow room for their employees' spiritual and cultural dimensions, and economies as a whole are similarly affected—if they are embedded in a context of social, cultural, and political freedom and responsibility. However, in the absence of a meaningful mission (which is the overarching ideal, as described by Peter Drucker), a joint vision and shared values, it appears that this consensus is becoming weaker in many countries. Instead, a self-interested approach is favored, with all its ineffectiveness, inefficiency and trust-destroying consequences for the economy, as well as for politics, culture and society—for mankind and its home. The answer lies in coevolution to the benefit of customers, employees, shareholders, and society, including our natural environment—shared value in the truest and best sense of the word.

The last word goes to Zhang Yue, founder of the Broad Group, Changsha:

> Being good itself is competitive. A bad company may be competitive in a market for a while, but it won't last long. If you offer something of social value, you will survive, and you will prosper. If everybody and every business becomes socially responsible, then the earth will become a beautiful hometown for us all. [108]

There are no limits to the benefits of coevolution.

---

[108] Alison Beard and Richard Hornik, "It's Hard to Be Good," *Harvard Business Review* (November 2011).

Epilogue
Coevolution Rather Than Greed or Free Prometheus!

Leadership is about how we shape futures
that we truly desire as opposed to try as
best we can to cope with circumstances
we believe are beyond our control.
—Peter Senge

The Corporate World: Under Pressure to Prove Its Legitimacy

Our corporate world is under pressure. It is increasingly being associated with problems in the economy itself, in the social sphere and in environmental issues, and there is much talk of privatizing profits while socializing the risks and losses. The corporate world is also facing a credibility problem; it is under great pressure to prove its legitimacy, and this is making its existence difficult.

The corporate world itself contributes considerably to this state of affairs—especially companies that operate under the narrow concept of value creation that has come into being over the past two or three decades. This approach is limited to short-term profit maximization for the company—and in the process, important aspects of long-term success remain hidden: long-term customer satisfaction and loyalty, sustainable employee motivation and retention, the preservation of natural resources that are vital to these companies, the performance of suppliers, and the interests and needs of the locations where companies engage in production and sales.

Guided by a narrowed understanding of value creation, the mistaken belief that economic success is incompatible with ethics and social progress is emerging to an ever greater degree. However, if the corporate world wants to regain trust and legitimacy and thus once again create an environment in which it can find long-lasting prosperity, the onus is on it to bring together business and society—and there are many wise, responsible, and prudent business owners and managers who know this. The concept of creating shared value, embedded in a meaning- and performance-centered corporate culture as it is embodied in the Value Balance in Business, opens up a way forward.

Free Prometheus!

The Value Balance in Business suggests a modern, contemporary theory of motivation as a starting point, instead of the concept of humanity presented by the standard theory of economics—that of maximization of self-interest—that still dominates today. For the past 150 years, economic thought and action have been determined by the dogma that the ultimate motive of human action is the direct pursuit of the greatest personal happiness or—in the business world—the pursuit of the greatest utility. According to this hypothesis, if people put this into practice they would be contributing toward the greatest happiness and the greatest benefit of the greatest number. This dogma went on to be hypostatized as a moral imperative for people and businesses.

The reader may remember that there is a problem with that: this motivation theory is wrong. Ironically, its founder, John Stuart Mill, had the good grace to withdraw this hypothesis himself. In his 1873 autobiography he wrote: "Ask yourself whether you are happy, and you cease to be so." In other words, if you pursue happiness, it will elude you. The utilitarian motivation theory of mainstream economics that is still dominant today does not work—it is a dead end, both for people and for businesses.

What is becoming clear from both meaning-centered psychology and a growing number of findings, especially in the field of evolutionary biology and neurobiology, is this: that which truly makes us humans what we are, and which therefore most fundamentally motivates us, is our seemingly unquenchable thirst for insight into the meaning of our actions and our functions, as well as our need to be appreciated as individuals, as the source of meaning for our existence. That is why we say: if you require people to perform, you have to offer them meaning and recognition in return. Where this is the case, employees are willing and able to grow beyond themselves and to give their best. It gives them a reason to be happy, and in the process happiness becomes a reality.

People find meaning in their deeds and actions, when these are not a (self-serving) end in themselves. Meaning is found when people place themselves at the service of others—customers, employees, supervisors, their own children, their partners, etc.—or when they perform tasks that are important for a larger circle of people. In doing so, people feel that they are "good for somebody" or "good for something," that they are recognized as individuals and have a rightful place in the world.

The more consistent companies are in placing themselves at the service of customers and society (i.e., when they are good for somebody or something, instead of pursuing merely selfish goals, such as short-term profit maximization), the more they expand their employees' horizon of meaning—and the more they reinforce employee motivation in the process. These employees realize that, through their company, they are doing something positive for customers and society; that they are able to participate in shaping our shared world, both actively and with joint responsibility. The result is that human labor undergoes a fundamental rehumanization, and there is a corresponding increase in the company's performance: "My goals, your goals, the company's goals are finally one and the same" (Gertrud Höhler).

We have come to know the *Homo economicus* of the self-interested standard theory of economics as a spiritless being. But it is the spiritual dimension of people that gives rise to the potential for creativity, innovation, and cooperation, and this is the most sustainable factor of all for progress, growth, and prosperity. The motivation theory of maximization of self-interest has put us in chains; the Value Balance in Business sets us free again—free Prometheus!

Coevolution: Economy and Society in Synergy

The second important aspect of a synergistic balance between the creation of economic and societal value is linked to the concept of creating shared value. For companies, shaping their business activity in such a way that they also contribute to the welfare of their local communities is not just good for employee motivation; it also makes sound economic sense. Cooperation with educational institutions or offering their own training programs results in skilled staff; an employment policy that regards layoffs only as a last resort and not merely as a means of short-term cost reduction preserves the expertise and loyalty of their employees and often that of their customers. Citizens who are remunerated fairly and have positive expectations for the future are good customers. Suppliers who are doing well and have substantial expertise are reliable and deliver high-quality products. Good direct relationships with raw material suppliers make companies independent of speculative bubbles. A wise procurement and location policy reduces transport costs and protects the environment. Production, packaging technologies, and storage solutions that make efficient use of resources reduce costs and benefit the environment over the long term. A healthy environment is in the interests of customers, employees, and their families, as well as being the source of essential, high-quality resources for many businesses. By adopting this approach, many companies find ways to set themselves apart in the market.

A third important aspect is that socially responsible companies enjoy a good reputation and the trust and loyalty of customers, employees, shareholders, media, the public, lenders, government, and politicians—all resources that help companies achieve long-lasting prosperity (and that remain inaccessible to self-interested companies). As employers, they are in high demand and can choose from the best people; thanks to their good reputation, they enjoy high levels of trust with lenders and government agencies and among the public; their customers are loyal, the brand is strong and profitable, and the employees are proud of their company and prepared to give their best for it and its customers.

In the long run, the state of the majority of companies cannot be separated from the state of society. It makes sense for companies to commit themselves to the welfare of those communities in which they operate, ultimately also in their own interests, but not with a focus on short-term maximization of self-interest. The free market can and must redefine itself and prosper beyond the primacy of self-interest—in a *synergistic* balance, creating economic and societal value for the benefit of customers, employees, shareholders, and society. By being there for each other in a spirit of coevolution, all parties can experience growth. Let us proceed from the point where mankind became truly human: in cooperation and the sharing of our resources, based on meaning and recognition.

Bibliography

Cited works

Anker, Heinrich. "Co-Evolution: Wealthier Together." In *Tendances économiques et sociales de la valeur en entreprise*, Valérie LeJeune. Paris: L'Harmattan, 2014.

Anker, Heinrich. *Ko-Evolution versus Eigennützigkeit* [Coevolution versus selfishness]. Berlin: Erich Schmidt Verlag, 2012.

Anker, H. *Balanced Valuecard: Leistung statt Egoismus* [Value balance in business performance rather than self-interest]. Bern: Verlag Haupt, 2010.

Anker, Heinrich. *Der Sinn im Ganzen: Bausteine einer praktischen Lebens- und Wirtschaftsethik* [Making sense of it all: building blocks for practical ethics for life and business]. Münster: ATE Verlag, 2004.

Antonovsky, Aaron, *Unraveling The Mystery of Health—How People Manage Stress and Stay Well*. San Francisco: Jossey-Bass Publishers, 1987.

Assagioli, Roberto, *Die Schulung des Willens* [Training of the will]. Paderborn: Junfermann, 2003.

Barton, Dominic. "Capitalism for the Long Term." *Harvard Business Review* (March 2011).

Bauer, Joachim. *Prinzip Menschlichkeit. Warum wir von Natur aus kooperieren* [The principle of humanity: why we naturally cooperate]. Hamburg: 2007 (5th ed.).

Beard, Alison, and Richard Hornik. "It's Hard to Be Good." *Harvard Business Review* (November 2011).

Bieri, Peter. "Was heisst es, über unser Leben selbst zu bestimmen?" [What does it mean to make decisions about our own lives?] *ZEIT Magazine,* no. 24 (July 2007), 49.

Bockstette, Valerie, and Mike Stamp. "Creating Shared Value: A How-to-Guide for the New Corporate (R)evolution," FSG, http://www.fsg.org/ ... /Creating-Shared-Value-A-How-to-Guide-for-the-New-Corporate-Revolution.aspx.

Böckmann, Walter. *Sinnorientierte Führung als Kunst der Motivation* [Meaning-oriented management and the art of motivation]. Landsberg/Lech: Verlag Moderne Industrie, 1987.

Clemmer Jim. *Moose on the Table: A Novel Approach to Communication at Work.* Toronto: Bastian Books, 2008.

Clemmer, Jim. *Leader's Digest: Timeless Principles for Team and Organization Success.* n.p.: TCG Press, 2003.

Clemmer, Jim. *Growing the Distance. Timeless Principles for Personal, Career, and Family Success.* n.p.:TCG Press, 1999.

Collins, Jim, and Morten T. Hansen. *Great by Choice: Uncertainty, Chaos and Luck—Why Some Thrive Despite Them All.* New York: Harper Business, 2011.

Collins, Jim. *How the Mighty Fall and Why Some Companies Never Give In.* New York: Harper Collins Publishers, 2009.

Collins, Jim. *Good to Great: Why Some Companies Make the Leap and Others Don't.* New York: Harper Business, 2001.

Collins, Jim, and Jerry I. Porras. *Built to Last: Successful Habits of Visionary Companies.* New York: Haper Business Essentials, 2002 (1994).

Drucker, Peter. *The Essential Drucker: Selections from the Management Works of Peter F. Drucker*, Classic Drucker Collection 2007 edition. Amsterdam etc.: Butterworth-Heinemann, 2007.

Ferrucci, Piero. *Nur die Freundlichen überleben. Warum wir lernen müssen, mit dem Herzen zu denken, wenn wir eine Zukunft haben wollen* [Only the kind survive. Why we must learn to think with our hearts if we want to have a future]. Berlin: Ullstein, 2006 (1st ed.).

Frankl, Viktor. *Der Mensch vor der Frage nach dem Sinn* [Mankind and the question of meaning]. Munich/Zurich: Piper, 1995 (10th ed.).

Frankl, Viktor. *Man's Search for Meaning.* New York: Washington Square Press, 1985.

Frankl, Viktor. *Der Wille zum Sinn* [The will to meaning: foundations and applications of logotherapy]. München: Piper, 1997 (4th ed.).

Frankl, Viktor. *Die Psychotherapie in der Praxis* [Psychotherapy in practice]. Munich / Zurich, 1995 (3rd ed.).

Friedman, M. "The Social Responsibility of Business Is to Increase Its Profits." *New York Times Magazine* (September 13, 1970): 32–33, 122, 124, 126.

Gallup. "Engagement Index Germany 2008." Marco Nink press conference, Potsdam, January 14, 2009.

Heskett, James. *The Culture Cycle. How to Shape the Unseen Force That Transforms Performance.* New Jersey: FT Press, 2012.

Hinterhuber, Hans. *Die 5 Gebote exzellenter Führung: Wie Ihr Untrernehmen in guten und in schlechten Zeiten zu den Gewinnern zählt* [The 5 commandments for excellent leadership: how your company can be a winner in good times and bad]. Frankfurt/Main: Frankfurter Allgemeine, 2010.

Höhler, Gertrud. *Die Sinnmacher: Wer siegen will, muss führen Berlin* [The meaning makers: If you want to win, you must lead]. Berlin: Econ, 2006 (2nd ed.).

Hüther, Gerald. *Bedienungsanleitung für ein menschliches Gehirn* [The compassionate brain: a revolutionary guide to developing your intelligence to its full potential]. Göttingen: Vandenhoek & Ruprecht, 2006 (6th ed.).

Isaksen, Jesper. "Constructing Meaning despite the Drudgery of Repetitive Work." *Journal of Humanistic Psychology* 40 (2000): 84–107.

Jaspers, Karl. *Was ist Philosophie?* [What is philosophy?] Munich: DTV, 1982.

Joyce, William, Nitin Nohria, and Bruce Roberson, *What (Really) Works: The 4+2 Formula for Sustained Business Success.* New York: Harper Business, 2003.

Kaku, Ryuzaburo. "The Path of Kyosei." *Harvard Business Review* 75 (July–August 1997): 55–63.

Kania, John, and Mark Kramer. "Q&A: Roundtable on Shared Value." *Stanford Social Innovation Review* (Summer 2011). http://www.fsg.org/tabid/191/ArticleId/359/Default.aspx? srpush=true.

Kaplan, Robert S., and David P. Norton. *Balanced Scorecard.* Stuttgart: Schäffer Poeschel, 1997.

Kay, John. *Obliquity: Why Our Goals Are Best Achieved Indirectly.* London: Profile Books, 2010.

Kelly Services. "Social responsibility key to attracting top talent." Media release. Troy, MI, October 28, 2009.

Kotter, John P., and James L. Heskett. *Corporate Culture and Performance.* New York: The Free Press, 1992.

Lukas, E. *Lehrbuch der Logotherapie* [Logotherapy textbook: meaning centered psychotherapy]. Munich/Vienna: Profil Verlag,1998.

Malik, Fredmund. "Konservativismus und effektives Management: Wege aus der Orientierungskrise" [Conservatism and effective management: ways out of the orientation crisis]. *In Kardinaltugenden effektiver Führung* [Cardinal virtues of effective management], edited by Peter Drucker and Peter Paschek. Frankfurt: Redline Wirtschaft, 2004.

Malik, Fredmund, *Führen, Leisten, Leben: Wirksames Management für eine neue Zeit* [Managing, performing, living: effective management for a new era]. Stuttgart/Munich: DVA, 2001 (10th ed.).

Meyer Schweizer, Ruth, Karl W. Haltiner, and Luca Bertossa. *Werte und Lebenschancen im Wandel. Eine Studie zu den Lebens-, Bildungs-, Arbeits- und Politikorientierungen junger Erwachsener in der Schweiz* [Values and life chances in transition: a study of the life, education, employment, and political orientations of young adults in Switzerland]. *Scientific Series* 19. Zurich/Chur: Rüegger, 2008.

Mill, John Stuart. *Autobiography.* London: Oxford University Press,1952 (1873).

Mill, John Stuart. *Utilitarianism.* London: Longmans, 1874 (5th ed.).

Mintzberg, Henry. *Inside Our Strange World of Organizations.* New York: The Free Press, 1989.

Neuweiler, Gerhard, *Und wir sind es doch—die Krone der Evolution* (We are it—the crown of evolution). Berlin: Wagenbach, 2009.

Peters, Thomas J., and Robert H. Waterman. *In Search of Excellence: Lessons from America's Best-Run Companies.* New York: Harper & Row, 1982.

Pircher-Friedrich, Anna Maria. *Mit Sinn zum nachhaltigen Erfolg: Anleitung zur werte—und wertorientierten Führung* [With meaning toward sustainable success: a guide to value and value-based management]. Berlin: Erich Schmidt Verlag, 2005.

Porter, Michael E., and Mark R. Kramer. "Creating Shared Value: How to Reinvent Capitalism—and Unleash a Wave of Innovation and Growth." *Harvard Business Review* (January–February 2011).

Porter, Michael E., and Mark R. Kramer. "Strategy & Society: The Link Between Competitive Advantage and Corporate Social Responsibility." *Harvard Business Review* (December 2006).

Rittmeyer, F. "Das war kurzfristig gedacht" [That was short-term thinking]. *Schweizer Monat*, no. 988 (July/August 2011): 49–52.

Sackmann, Sonja A. *Assessment, Evaluation, Improvement: Success through Corporate Culture*. Gütersloh: Verlag Bertelsmann Stiftung, 2006.

Schein, Edgar H. *Organizational Culture and Leadership*. San Francisco: Jossey-Bass, 2004 (3rd ed.).

Schnell, Tatjana. "The Sources of Meaning and Meaning in Life Questionnaire (SoME): Relations to Demographics and Well-Being." *Journal of Positive Psychology* 4, no. 6 (2009): 483–499.

Smith, Adam. *Theorie der ethischen Gefühle* [Theory of moral sentiments]. Hamburg: Felix Meiner Verlag, 1985.

Sprenger, Reinhard K. *Mythos Motivation: Wege aus einer Sackgasse* [The motivation of myth: a way out of the dead-end street). Frankfurt/New York: Campus, 1999 (16th ed.).

Wallimann, Isidor, and Esteban Piñeiro. *Sozialpolitik nach dem Verursacherprinzip* [Social policy according to the polluter pays principle: examples of application in the field of addiction, obesity, abuse of medicine, unemployment, prostitution]. Munich: 2011.

Wallimann, Isidor. *Sozialpolitik anders denken: Das Verursacherprinzip—von der umweltpolitischen zur sozialpolitischen Anwendung* [Social policy from another perspective: causal agency and responsibility]. http://books.google.com/books?id=yn4yQuS9HAYC&printsec=frontcover&dq=sozialpolitik+anders+denken&hl=de&ei=gZPjTdjDAcmZOr6lvLcG&sa=X&oi=book_result&ct=result&resnum=1&ved=0CCoQ6AEwAA#v=onepage&q&f=false.

Wilkinson, R., and K. Pickett. *The Spirit Level: Why Equality Is Better for Everyone*. London: Penguin Books, 2010 (2009).

Young, Stephen. *Moral Capitalism: Reconciling Private Interest with the Public Good*. San Francisco: Berrett-Koehler, 2003.

Zika, Sheryl and Kerry Chamberlain. "On the Relation between Meaning in Life and Psychological Well-Being." *British Journal of Psychology* (1992): 133–145.

zur Bonsen, Matthias. *Leading with Life: Lebendigkeit im Unternehmen freisetzen und nutzen* [Leading with life: releasing and using vitality in companies]. Wiesbaden: Gabler 2009 (1st ed.).

Further reading

Anker, Heinrich. "Verantwortung oder Zuckerwatte? Der Einzelne und die Krise" [Responsibility or cotton candy? The individual and crisis]. *Der Bund* (Monday, October 27 2008): 2.

Anker, Heinrich, and Marcella G. Haensch."Passt das Gesamtpaket? Unternehmenskultur auf dem Prüfstand" [Does the whole package fit? Putting corporate culture to the test]. *Alpha—Der Kadermarkt der Schweiz* [Alpha—The executive market in Switzerland] (Saturday, May 18, 2009): 4.

Bauer, Joachim. *Lob der Schule. Sieben Perspektiven für Schüler, Lehrer und Eltern* [In praise of school: seven perspectives for pupils, teachers, and parents]. Munich: Hoffmann und Campe, 2008 (2nd ed.).

Bauer, Joachim. *Warum ich fühle, was du fühlst. Intuitive Kommunikation und das Geheimnis der Spiegelneurone* [Why I feel what you feel. intuitive communication and the secret of mirror neurons]. München: Wilhelm Heyne Verlag, 2006 (5th ed.).

Bauer, Joachim. *Das Gedächtnis des Körpers: Wie Beziehungen und Lebensstile unsere Gene steuern* [The body's memory: how relationships and lifestyles control our genes]. Frankfurt/Main: Eichborn, 2002.

Becker, Ernest. *The Denial of Death.* New York: The Free Press, 1973.

Böckmann, Walter. *Vom Sinn zum Gewinn* [From meaning to profit]. Wiesbaden: Gabler, 1990.

Brandmeyer, Klaus, et al. *Marken stark machen: Techniken der Markenführung* [Creating strong brands: techniques in branding]. Weinheim: Wiley VCH Verlag, 2008.

Bruckner, Pascal. *Verdammt zum Glück: Der Fluch der Moderne* [Condemned to joy: the Western cult of happiness is a mirthless enterprise]. Berlin: Aufbau Verlag, 2002 (2001).

Christensen, Clayton M., and Michael E. Raynor. *The Innovator's Solution: Creating and Sustaining Successful Growth.* Boston: Harvard Business School Press, 2003.

Chun, Rosa, and Gary Davies. "Employees' Happiness Isn't Enough to Satisfy Customers." *Harvard Business Review* (April 2009).

Covey, Stephen M. R. *The Speed of Trust: The One Thing That Changes Everything.* New York: Free Press, 2006.

Dahrendorf, Ralph. "Verantwortlicher Kapitalismus" [Responsible capitalism]. *Finanz und Wirtschaft* [Finance and economy] 74, no. 91 (Wednesday, November 21, 2001): 1.

Diller, Steve, Nathan Shedroff, and Darrel Rhea. *Making Meaning: How Successful Businesses Deliver Meaningful Customer Experiences.* Berkeley: New Riders, 2006.

Domizlaff, Hans. *Die Gewinnung des öffentlichen Vertrauens: Ein Lehrbuch der Markentechnik* [Regaining the public's trust: a textbook for techniques in branding]. Hamburg: Marketing Journal, 1992.

Einstein, Albert. *Mein Weltbild* [The world as I see it]. Edited by Carl Seelig. Frankfurt am Main/Berlin: Ullstein, 1988.

Esch, Franz-Rudolf. *Strategie und Technik der Markenführung* [Strategy and techniques of brand management]. Munich: Vahlen, 2008 (5th ed.).

Ferrucci, Piero. *Werde was Du bist: Selbstverwirklichung durch Psychosynthese* [What we may be: techniques for psychological and spiritual growth through psychosynthesis]. Hamburg: Rohwolt Taschenbuch Verlag, 2002 (1986).

Frankl, Viktor. *Logotherapie und Existenzanalyse: Texte aus sechs Jahrzehnten* [Logotherapy and existential analysis. texts from six decades]. Weinheim: Beltz Psychologie Verlags Union, 1998 (3rd ed.).

Frankl, Viktor. Ärztliche Seelsorge*: Grundlagen der Logotherapie und Existenzanalyse* [The doctor and the soul: from psychotherapy to logotherapy]. Frankfurt: Fischer Taschenbuch Verlag GmbH, 1997.

Frankl, Viktor. *Die Sinnfrage in der Psychotherapie* [The question of meaning in psychotherapy]. München/ Zürich: Piper, 1996 (6th ed.).

Frankl, Viktor. *Der leidende Mensch: Anthropologische Grundlagen der Psychotherapie* [The suffering human: anthropological foundations of psychotherapy]. Bern/Göttingen/Toronto/Seattle: Verlag Hans Huber, 1996 (2nd ed.).

Gälweiler, Aloys, *Strategische Unternehmensführung* [Strategic corporate management]. Frankfurt am Main: Campus 2005 (3rd ed.).

Gauthier, Alain. *Le co-leadership évolutionnaire pour une société co-créatrice en émergence*. Auxerre: HD Précursions, 2013.

Geertz, Clifford. *The Interpretation of Culture*. New York: Basic Books, 1973.

Handy, Charles. *The Hungry Spirit*. London: Arrow, 2002.

Heuser, Jean. "Die unterschätzte Macht der Ökonomen" [The underestimated power of the economists]. *Die Zeit*, no. 48 (November 23, 2006): 33.

Hüther, Gerald. *Die Macht der inneren Bilder: Wie Visionen das Gehirn, den Menschen und die Welt verändern* [The power of mental images: how visions change the brain, people, and the world]. Göttingen: Vandenhoeck & Ruprecht, 2006.

Hüther, Gerald. *Die Evolution der Liebe: Was Darwin bereits ahnte und die Darwinisten nicht wahrhaben wollen* [The evolution of love: what Darwin already suspected and Darwinists don't want to admit]. Göttingen: Vandenhoeck & Ruprecht, 2003 (3rd ed.).

Kirby, Julia. "Toward a Theory of High Performance." *Harvard Business Review* (July–August 2005).

Krähenbühl, Niklaus. "Darf man die Kräfte im Markt verzetteln?" [May we dissipate the market forces?]. *io Management Zeitschrift* 58, no. 1 (1989): 52–55.

Krähenbühl, Niklaus. "Ein humaner Führungsansatz—und deshalb gerade für kleinere Firmen erfolgreich" [A humane approach to leadership—and therefore particularly successful for smaller companies]. *io Management Zeitschrift* 51, no. 2 (1982): 84.

Malik, Fredmund. "Gewinn—bestens bekannt und doch unverstanden" [Profit—so well known, so little understood]. *M.o.M. Malik on Management*, no. (2001): 118f.

March, James. "Der Meister der Ideen" [The master of ideas]. *Harvard Business Manager* (February 2007): 105–111.

Marquard, Odo. *Philosophie des Stattdessen* [Philosophy of the instead]. Stuttgart: Philipp Reclam jun.,2000.

Maucher, Helmut. Interview. *persönlich* (December 2001): 10f.

Maucher, Helmut, *Management Brevier. Ein Leitfaden für unternehmerischen Erfolg* [Management breviary: a guide to success in business]. Frankfurt/New York: Campus, 2007.

Mayo, Elton. *The Human Problems of an Industrial Civilization*. New York: 1933.

Mintzberg, Henry, Bruce Ahlstrand, and Joseph Lampel. *Strategy Safari: Eine Reise durch die Wildnis des strategischen Managements* [Strategy safari: a guided tour through the wilds of strategic management]. Heidelberg: Redline Wirtschaft, 2007.

O'Hallaron, Richard, and David O'Hallaron. *The Mission Primer: Four Steps to an Effective Mission Statement*. Richmond: Mission Incorporated, 2009.

Pattakos, Alex. *Prisoners of Our Thoughts: Viktor Frankl's Principles for Discovering Meaning in Life and Work*. San Francisco: Berrett-Koehler, 2004.

Percy, Ian. *Going Deep: Exploring Spirituality in Life and Leadership*. Toronto: Macmillan Canada, 1997.

Pircher-Friedrich, Anna Maria, and Rolf Klaus Friedrich. *Gesundheit, Erfolg und Erfüllung: Eine Anleitung—auch für Manager* [Health, success and fulfillment: a guide—also for managers]. Berlin: Erich Schmidt Verlag, 2009.

Porath, Christine, and Christine Pearson. "How Toxic Colleagues Corrode Performance." *Harvard Business Review* (April 2009).

Prahalad, C. K., and Gary Hamel. "The Core Competence of the Corporation." *Harvard Business Review* (May–June 1990): 79–91.

Raynor, Michael E., Mumtaz Ahmed, and Andrew D. Henderson. "Are 'Great' Companies Just Lucky?" *Harvard Business Review* (April 2009).

Riemeyer, Jörg. *Die Logotherapie Viktor Frankls: Eine Einführung in die sinnorientierte Psychotherapie* [Viktor Frankl's logotherapy: an introduction to meaning-oriented psychotherapy]. Gütersloh: Quell Verlag, 2002 (2nd ed.).

Sackmann, Sonja. *Erfolgsfaktor Unternehmenskultur: Mit kulturbewusstem Management Unternehmensziele erreichen und Identifikation schaffen—6 Best Practice-Beispiele* [Success factor: corporate culture: developing a corporate culture for high performance and long-term competitiveness, six best practices]. Wiesbaden: Gabler, 2004.

Schlesinger, Leonard A., and James L. Heskett. "The Service-Driven Company." *Harvard Business Review* (September–October 1991): 15.

Schumpeter, Joseph A. *Geschichte der ökonomischen Analyse (Grundriss der Sozialwissenschaft, Bd. 6)* [The history of economic analysis. (Outline of social sciences, vol. 6)]. Göttingen: Vandenhoeck & Ruprecht, 1965.

Schumpeter, Joseph A. *Capitalism, Socialism, and Democracy*. New York: Harper, 1942.

Senge, Peter M. *The Fifth Discipline. The Art and Practice of the Learning Organization*. New York: Doubleday, 1990.

Smith, Adam. *Der Wohlstand der Nationen. Eine Untersuchung seiner Natur und seiner Ursachen* [Inquiry into the nature and causes of the wealth of nations]. Munich: Beck, 1974.

Ulrich, Dave, and Norm Smallwood. "Building a Leadership Brand." *Harvard Business Review* (July–August 2007).

Ulwick, Anthony W. "Turn Customer Input in Innovation." *Harvard Business Review* (January 2002).

Von Hayek, Friedrich August. "Der Wettbewerb als Entdeckungsverfahren" [Competition as a discovery procedure]. In *Freiburger Studien*. Tübingen: 1969.

Watzlawick, Paul, Janet H. Beavin, and Don D. Jackson. *Menschliche Kommunikation: Formen, Störungen, Paradoxien* [Human communication: forms, interference, paradoxes]. 9th edition. Bern/Stuttgart/Toronto: Verlag Hans Huber, 1996.

Index

pragmatic ethics, 156–157n102
products and services, as Perspective
5 of Value Balance in Business
audit, 110–111
professional expertise, 152–153
profit maximization, 162, 164t–166t.
See also short-term, profit
maximization
profitability, as increasing when
companies consistently serve
clients and society above all
else, 3–4
Prost, Winfried, 101
psychological commitment, 102

Q

quality management, 22f

R

reason for existence (of company), 102
recognition
as avenue toward meaning, 53, 53f,
54–55, 62
as core component of Value Balance
in Business, 101
as existential need, 2, 35, 39, 44, 51,
96f–97f, 98
internal communication as
facilitator of, 88–89
recruitment, taking mission, vision, and
values into consideration in, 151
relationship values, 64
reputation (of company), 81–85, 116
responsibility, as primal human
ability, 24
Ricola, 67, 68, 76, 82
Roberson, B., 16, 26, 43, 77, 87

S

Schein, Edgar, 93, 95
Scheler, Max, 30, 32f
scientific management, 29, 30

scores (of Value Balance in Business
audit), tracking of, 138–142,
140t–141t
self-actualization, 74
self-awareness, 31
self-conscious, humans as, 34
self-distancing, 32–34, 105
self-fulfilling prophecies, 93, 94
self-identity, 34, 35, 35n33
self-interest, 9, 11–20, 24–26, 30, 33, 36,
49, 50f, 57, 72, 95, 96f–97f, 98,
156, 162, 163, 164t–166t, 170
self-realization, 74, 76, 113t, 164t
self-transcendence/self-transcendent, 31,
38–39, 65t, 66, 72, 85, 160
Seligman, Martin, 93
Senge, Peter, 169
service entities, companies as, 23
Seveso dioxin disaster, 11
shared value
creation of. *See* creating shared
value (CSV)
optimal context for, 58
shared-value approach, 9, 10, 13, 14,
68, 98
shareholders, as Perspective 8 of Value
Balance in Business audit, 117
short-term
approach, 163
benefit, 1
buildup in growth, 163
cost calculations/considerations,
24, 82
cost reduction, 172
financial performance, 7
gain, xi, 12, 16, 18
profit maximization, 3, 4, 13, 15, 22,
24, 36, 60, 61, 68, 72, 84, 88,
98, 115n94, 163, 169, 172, 173
reduction of employees, physical
capital, and customer
relations/services, 163
self-interest, 3, 4
shareholder value, 16, 28
view, 162

194

Open Book Editions
A Berrett-Koehler Partner

Open Book Editions is a joint venture between Berrett-Koehler Publishers and Author Solutions, the market leader in self-publishing. There are many more aspiring authors who share Berrett-Koehler's mission than we can sustainably publish. To serve these authors, Open Book Editions offers a comprehensive self-publishing opportunity.

A Shared Mission

Open Book Editions welcomes authors who share the Berrett-Koehler mission—Creating a World That Works for All. We believe that to truly create a better world, action is needed at all levels—individual, organizational, and societal. At the individual level, our publications help people align their lives with their values and with their aspirations for a better world. At the organizational level, we promote progressive leadership and management practices, socially responsible approaches to business, and humane and effective organizations. At the societal level, we publish content that advances social and economic justice, shared prosperity, sustainability, and new solutions to national and global issues.

Open Book Editions represents a new way to further the BK mission and expand our community. We look forward to helping more authors challenge conventional thinking, introduce new ideas, and foster positive change.

For more information, see the Open Book Editions website:
http://www.iuniverse.com/Packages/OpenBookEditions.aspx

Join the BK Community! See exclusive author videos, join discussion groups, find out about upcoming events, read author blogs, and much more! http://bkcommunity.com/

Printed in the United States
By Bookmasters